LATHROP
MONROE ST.
HENRY
CLINTON
IRVING
IRVING PLACE
MENOMONEE
ELIZABETH ST.
ANN ST.
WALNUT ST.
FOREST AVE.
ELIZABETH COURT
ST.
LUELLA
GROVE AVE.
WILLIS ST.
CHICAGO AVE.
PARK
AVE.
VIEW OF
PARK
7 PUBLIC SCHOOL
8 HARLEM PUBLIC SCHOOL
9 HOTEL
10 DEPOT
11 N.W.R.R. SHOPS
12 HARLEM HOUSE

We dedicate this book to the people of Oak Park — past and present — whose faith, determination and courage helped to build a strong foundation for our village's progress and growth — and in so doing made it a fine place to live, work, and play.

We hope this beautifully illustrated and well-documented volume will prove to be a cherished addition to your family library as well as a rare collector's item in years to come. Suburban Trust and Savings Bank is proud to have played a vital, long-standing role in our community's heritage and growth.

On behalf of the Board of Directors, officers and employees of Suburban Trust and Savings Bank, we are pleased to present to our customers and friends this limited edition copy of OAK PARK: A PICTORIAL HISTORY.

Denis J. Daly
Chairman of the Board and Chief Executive Officer
SUBURBAN TRUST AND SAVINGS BANK

GOLDEN JUBILEE
GOLDEN JUBILEE
GOLDEN JUBILEE
SUN. - SAT. - AUG. 19 - 25
OAK PARK "GOLDEN JUBILEE"
OAK PARK HIGH SCHOOL STADIUM

OAK PARK

A PICTORIAL HISTORY

BY

JEAN GUARINO

G. BRADLEY PUBLISHING, INC
ST. LOUIS, MISSOURI

OAK PARK

A PICTORIAL HISTORY

by

Jean Guarino

A Limited Edition
of 3000
of which this is

NUMBER _______________

PUBLICATION STAFF:
AUTHOR: Jean Guarino
ADVISORS: Elsie Jacobsen
Carol Kelm
COVER ARTIST: Ruth Reinel
BOOK DESIGN: IPC Graphics-George F. Lestina
Carol Dunn-Art Director
Michael Gartland-Production
COPY EDITOR: Ellen Kim
PUBLISHER: G. Bradley Publishing, Inc.
SPONSOR: Suburban Trust and Savings Bank

All photos are courtesy of the Oak Park and River Forest Historical Society unless otherwise noted.

ISBN 0-943963-06-0
Printed in the United States of America

TABLE OF CONTENTS

FOREWORD

For many people the most interesting and relaxing way to study history is to analyze early photographs. These visual, historic records are actually mini time capsules that freeze the personalities, events and landmarks of the past. Photos give us the power to be select observers to the passage of time. We realize that what we take for granted today was once more difficult and much different.

Within the pages of *Oak Park: A Pictorial History* the rich history of our community comes visually alive through photographs. Well-documented by local history buff, Jean Guarino, *Oak Park: A Pictorial History* is a book full of fact, legend and lore. From Joseph Kettlestrings, the first settler, to the residents of today, we see the history of a community that wants the best for its citizens. Oak Park leaders have continually tried to shape the future of their community and not let its destiny be controlled by outside influences.

Historic preservation is progress, too. Knowing the strength of our community's roots binds us and lends even greater confidence to the stability and aspirations of our future. In *Oak Park: A Pictorial History* you will share in the excitement and vitality of a city on the grow. It is a book and a knowledge you will always cherish.

Joseph Kettlestrings, Oak Park's first settler who built a small frame home in 1835 on the site of what is now Walgreen's drug store on Lake Street. Kettlestrings was also the village's first innkeeper offering hospitality to travelers making the journey to and from Chicago over roads that were little more than rough trails often mired in mud.

Kettlestrings Grove, as the quarter section he purchased came to be known, was bounded by what is today Chicago Avenue, Oak Park Avenue, the North Western tracks, and Harlem Avenue. By the 1850s the tiny community of Oak Ridge began to grow as Kettlestrings subdivided and sold his land to "good people who were against saloons and for good schools and churches."

Betty Kettlestrings, who left her Yorkshire home in 1833 with her husband Joseph and their two small children to settle on a tract of government land in a frontier town called Chicago. Once here the Kettlestrings bypassed Chicago and pushed eight and a half miles further west until they came to the first dry land they had seen in weeks, a broad-topped ridge in a forest of oaks.

Here the family rested and Betty informed her husband, "Joseph, this is as far as we go." He agreed, and surveyed and laid claim to a 172 acre tract that included this "oak ridge."

Betty Kettlestrings endured the hardships shared by other pioneer women including illness, mud, marauding Indians and wild animals. She had eleven children but lost four to Scarlet Fever and other illnesses.

A copy of the government deed which conveys 172.78 acres of land from the federal government, under the provisions of the Public Lands Sale Act of 1820, to Joseph Kettlestrings for $215.98 or approximately $1.25 an acre.

Although the land wasn't deeded to Kettlestrings until 1837, he lived on it as early as 1835 when the government opened the land for pre-emption and allowed settlers to live on it as 'squatters' until it was offered for sale.

CHAPTER I

THE
PIONEERING
YEARS

1833-1871

The early history of Oak Park, like that of other midwest towns and villages carved out of the prairies, is the story of both the adventures and exploits as well as the trials and difficulties experienced by a resourceful group of pioneers who left their homes to settle in Oak Ridge.

Land, rich farm land and plenty of it, sold at bargain prices by the federal government, was the thing that lured most settlers. They arrived here in their prairie schooners and farm wagons expecting hardship and they were not disappointed. But neither were they disappointed by what they received in return — the opportunity to purchase large parcels of land and to do with it as they chose.

The geologic composition of the land plays an important role in Oak Park's history. The foundation beneath the village is formed by three strata, the first of limestone, the second a rubber-like mat of glacial drift, the third a so-called spit or ridge of sand thrown up on the shores of a large lake which geologists refer to as "Lake Chicago."

As the ice from the last glacial age melted, it formed this inland sea which lay over Oak Park and River Forest and stood 60 feet higher than Lake Michigan does today, with an elevation of 580 feet.

This spit or ridge runs diagonally from what is now the corner of Ridgeland and North Avenue on the northeast, leveling out gradually to the southwest and ending near Madison Street and Des Plaines Avenue where it is scarcely noticeable.

Today, worn down by grading and building, the ridge has practically disappeared except in the southern slope of what is now Scoville Park and in Taylor Park at Ridgeland and Division. More than 150 years ago, though, this ridge was more pronounced, with an almost continuous forest of oak trees along its crest which gave the region its old name of Oak Ridge.

The history of Oak Park can be traced as far back as 1673 when Marquette and Joliet traversed the Aux Plaines River (today known as the Des Plaines River). At that time the site of Oak Park was a wilderness inhabited by tribes of Pottawatomie, Sac and Fox Indians.

When Illinois was admitted to the Union in November, 1818, the state was divided into fourteen counties with the site of Oak Park located in what was then Crawford County.

But in 1831 the Illinois legislature changed the boundaries and names of Illinois counties and two years later, when Kettlestrings made his claim of 125 acres, the site of what was to become Oak Park was in Cook County.

In 1835 when Joseph Kettlestrings built a drafty cabin of oak boards for his family in this timbered and prairie wilderness, Chicago, a growing community of homes clustered around Fort Dearborn, already had a population of about 350.

These settlers, soldiers, entrepreneurs and adventurers banded together for mutual protection and so were able to withstand perils that included mud, marauding Indians, wild animals and sickness.

More enterprising pioneers like Joseph Kettlestrings were willing to leave the security of the small fort on the bank of the Chicago River for the opportunity to purchase large tracts of land at bargain prices from the federal government under the Public Lands Sale Act of 1820.

Joseph Kettlestrings was born in Newton, Yorkshire, England in 1808. In 1828 he married Betty Willis and in 1832 the Kettlestringses with their two small children, migrated to America with the intention of settling on a tract of government land in a frontier town called Chicago.

Two years earlier a neighbor, George Bickerdike, had come to this new country and written glowing accounts of Chicago — and of the rich timber land not so many miles to the west. But when the family reached Chicago from Cincinnati in a covered wagon, they found reality bore little resemblance to their friend's idyllic description.

Chicago, at that time, was a quagmire of mud and consisted of an array of unpainted frame houses set in a sea of puddles, pools, bogs and sloughs and lashed by dreary, unceasing rains. It was hard to believe the sun ever shone here and the Kettlestringses didn't wait to see. Instead, they pushed on further west for another eight and a half miles.

And so, in the spring of 1833, on a heavily wooded and broad-topped ridge (in what is now Scoville Park) the Kettlestringeses found the first dry land they had seen in more than two weeks. The forests of oak and beech trees reminded them of the English forests they had left behind and they knew this was the end of their journey.

Kettlestrings selected and surveyed a claim in Oak Ridge but did not settle on it immediately. Instead, he moved his family into a log cabin one mile further west on the banks of the Des Plaines River. Here his friend George Bickerdike and another Yorkshireman, Mark Noble, had set up a saw mill. Kettlestrings bought an interest in the mill and spent the next two years operating it with his friends.

In 1835 Kettlestrings returned to his claim and built a small frame house on the site of what is now Walgreen's drug store on Lake Street, and so became Oak Park's first settler. The house was made of oak lumber from the mill, and after it had withstood the first summer's heat, the clapboards curled up and they had to stuff the cracks with rags and paper as winter arrived.

Under the provisions of the Public Lands Sale Act of 1820, Kettlestrings purchased 172.78 acres from the federal government for $215.98, or approximately $1.25 an acre. The deed to this quarter section eventually known as Kettlestrings Grove was signed in Washington, D.C. on March 20, 1837 and arrived in Oak Ridge on March 30, 1837.

Kettlestrings' quarter section was established by original survey and was bounded by what is today Chicago Avenue, Oak Park Avenue, the North Western tacks and Harlem Avenue, all boundaries that were set by original survey as section lines.

According to Walter Kettlestrings, his father did not stop with this initial purchase of land but later bought 160 acres north of Chicago Avenue and another 80 acres running both north and south of the village itself. With an eye for settling the land, Kettlestrings enclosed his original 172 acres in Oak Ridge with a rail fence.

Although the land wasn't deeded to Kettlestrings until 1837 he was able to live on it as early as 1835 when the government opened the land for pre-emption and allowed settlers to live on it as "squatters" until it was offered for sale.

For a number of years the Kettlestrings' home was the only

habitation between the city and the few homes on the Des Plaines River, and so they offered hospitality to weary travelers making the journey. There were no sleeping rooms but visitors were welcome to spread their blankets on the floor in front of the blazing logs and partake of Betty Kettlestrings' plain and often frugal board.

As the number of visitors increased, however, Kettlestrings built a small addition and put a price upon his hospitality. He gave travelers supper, breakfast, and lodging and charged them 50 cents. Although this lodging was called "tavern" Kettlestrings never sold liquor, and in later years joined H. W. Austin, Sr. in banning it from the community.

By 1843 there were a few more houses in Kettlestrings Grove. There were also Indians and rattlesnakes, about which one of the daughters reminisced, "we knew not which we feared most." Probably the rattlesnakes, for Mrs. Kettlestrings once killed one in her kitchen.

At this point schools had yet to be established in Oak Ridge. As a result Kettlestrings rented his farm and moved to Chicago for the next 12 years so his children could be educated. Chicago was experiencing rapid expansion, so Kettlestrings bought a team of horses, obtained city contracts, and went into business grading streets.

When the Kettlestrings family returned to Oak Park in 1855, Joseph Kettlestrings retired from business and began selling portions of his extensive holdings. He sold his farm and built a new home in the center of what is now Grove Avenue, facing Lake Street. When Grove was made a street this house was moved to Scoville and Lake. It was not demolished until 1935 when it stood in the path of an expansion at the high school.

Whenever Kettlestrings sold a lot and the purchaser was unable to meet the payment, he took the property back and returned whatever sum had been paid, less interest. When he drew up a deed he always inserted a clause which bound the purchaser never to sell intoxicating liquor on the premises.

By the 1850s and 60s, the tiny community of Oak Ridge began to grow as the result of the sale and subsequent subdividing of Kettlestrings' land. The small enclave between Oak Park Avenue and Harlem Avenue contained several dozen stores and homes owned by businessmen, bankers, teachers and storekeepers with names like Austin, Gale, Bolles, Herrick, Niles, Dunlop and Scoville.

In 1855 Kettlestrings donated a lot on the northwest corner of Lake and Forest for a nondescript frame building that was to play several leading roles in Oak Park's history. The building was originally used as the village's first school between 1857 and 1859. Later it was known as the "Mother of Churches" when it served as the first church for the God-fearing community. And finally, renamed Temperance Hall, it became a temple dedicated to sobriety by H. W. Austin, Sr. and his supporters who were responsible for the 1872 law banning the sale of liquor in the area.

During this period Oak Ridge and the surrounding area was governed by the Cicero Township Board. When Chicago was incorporated in 1837 the remainder of Cook County was left with an indefinite form of government until 1857, when the Township of Cicero was established. The elected Township Board was responsible for governing Austin, Ridgeland, Cicero, Berwyn, Oak Ridge, and a few other small settlements.

Today villagers recognize "Ridgeland" as the name of a major thoroughfare in Oak Park, but few realize that when this portion of Cook County was governed by the Cicero Town Board, Ridgeland was a town separate from Oak Ridge.

This large tract in what is now the eastern portion of the village, was located north of the North Western tracks and as far west as East Avenue. The land has been purchased for $700 an acre by James Scoville, W. B. Ogden, Joel D. Harvey and Josiah Lombard, for whom some of the streets are now named.

E. A. Cummings, a local real estate entrepreneur with an eye for a bargain, settled in the area in 1869 and subdivided the area in 1872. Ridgeland, as it came to be known, became a prosperous community. The center of this town's social life was a brick community hall on Lake near Ridgeland.

Anyone attempting to trace the growth of Oak Park has only to follow the expansion of the railroad west from Chicago. Like the old Indian trails and the roads opened by prairie schooners, the railroad was the conduit that made Oak Park a suburb of Chicago and helped attract new residents.

In 1848 the Galena and Chicago Union Railroad, the first to run west of Chicago, laid its tracks through Oak Ridge built a station just west of Harlem Avenue in what is now River Forest and named it Harlem Station. There were only two freight trains per day going both east and west and each was trailed by a caboose.

The story is told that James Scoville was often the only passenger to enjoy the caboose for the hour's ride each way to and from the city. The railroad later added a passenger car, and became the first commuter train serving travelers on a road that extended only 21 miles west of Chicago. In 1864 the Chicago and North Western purchased the Chicago and Galena Union Railroad and increased the service, with special emphasis on commuter service to the city.

As the number of residents commuting to Chicago continued to grow there was a demand for a station in Oak Park, but the citizens of Harlem were unwilling to give up their station. A court suit was pending, so a group of Oak Parkers had an amicable interview with railway officials, and it was decided that the easiest way was the best way.

In the early morning darkness of April 20, 1872, the small depot (which was a baggage car with the wheels removed) was slid down the tracks between two engines to a spot just east of Marion St. The new sign on the small station proclaimed it to be "Oak Park."

This name was selected to match that of the post office which had been named "Oak Park" a year earlier, when it was moved to O. W. Herrick's general store on Lake Street from a drug store on Lake Street just west of the Des Plaines River bridge in Harlem (now the site of McDonald's).

The post office was called Oak Park because the names "Harlem" and "Oak Ridge" had already been assigned to other post offices in the state. As a compromise the name Oak Park was chosen. So, between the post office and the railroad station, the name Oak Ridge was dropped and, in 1872, Oak Park became the official name of the community.

But while a new name marked a milestone in this small village, another event which occurred a year earlier had an even greater impact. The catastrophic Chicago Fire of 1871, which all but leveled the city, created a boom in Oak Park land values as many Chicagoans decided to rebuild in the suburbs.

As a result, between 1870 and 1890, Oak Park gradually changed from an obscure country town to a thriving suburb. The population which was approximately 500 in 1870 more than doubled in the year after the fire, and is given as 4,589 in the 1890 school census. Large frame homes were built and many of the original settler's modest homes were torn down to make room for larger and more pretentious ones. Land which Kettlestrings had purchased for $1.25 an acre in 1835 sold for $1,000 an acre in 1871 and for $3,000 an acre three years later.

The Steiner building, 101 Lake Street, on the northeast corner of Lake and Harlem, was Oak Park's first grocery and dry goods store. It was established in 1856 by a Mr. Furbeck, who sold it two years later to Mrs. Catherine Pattock, who ran it alone until she married William Steiner. Old timers recalled Mrs. Steiner sitting in front of the store knitting — and keeping a keen eye out for customers. The Steiners later built a more substantial brick building at Lake and Marion on the site of Park Square.

The Steiner building is a good example of the reverse numbering system that was used on Lake Street between Harlem and Austin Blvd. until about 1902. The east to west numbering that ran east from Harlem to Austin was later changed to run in the opposite direction, west to east from Austin to Harlem. Hence, the Steiner building which was numbered 101 Lake would today be 1144 Lake.

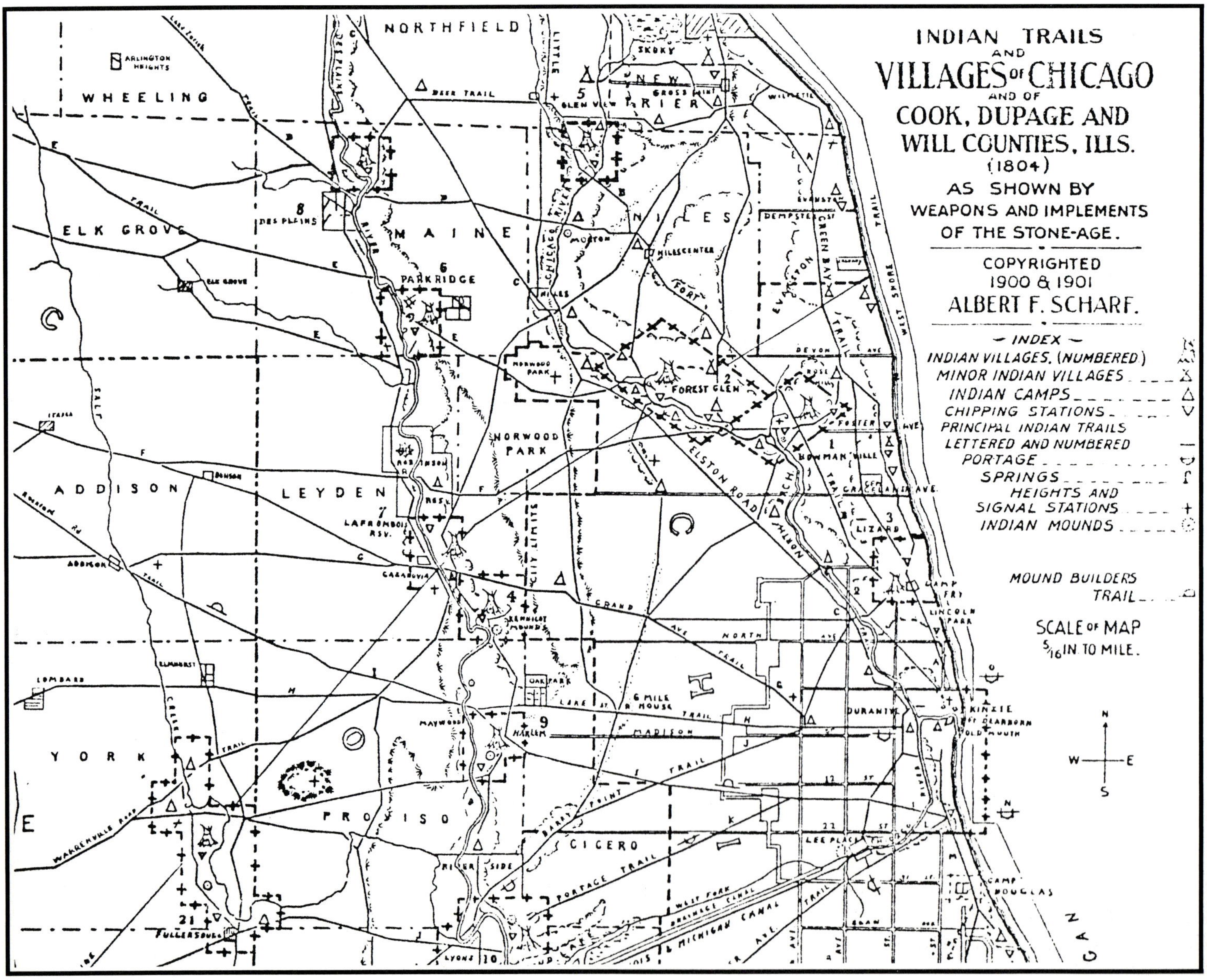

William Waters, considered one of the best "shoe men" in the business, working on a customer's horse.

In 1872 William Johnston opened this carriage making business and blacksmith shop at 121-3 Lake Street near Harlem Ave. Some of the different types of carriages and wagons made in the shop are displayed in front.

Note that the building on the right of Johnston's belonged to Frank Ellis, a master carpenter who, like so many other villagers, came here from New York state. Ellis established a successful contracting and building business in 1871. Although he had no formal architectural training, he, and not Frank Lloyd Wright, is considered Oak Park's first architect because he designed and built so many prominent buildings.

Star Bright Livery, one of the pioneer livery and boarding stables in the village, was located on what is now the site of Grace Episcopal Church, 924 Lake. This view is looking southeast from Ontario Street.

The first drug store and doctor's office was opened in Oak Park by Orin Peake, who is pictured here in front of the three story brick building he built in 1873, at 206 (now 1051) Lake Street. The "O. P." on the storefront window stood for Orin Peake and not for Oak Park.

Dr. Peake helped compile the first village directory. In 1885 he opened a registry in his store and asked all citizens to stop in and record their name and address. This was the basis for the first village directory which was published in 1886 and every year thereafter. After his retirement, Dr. Peake was an active member of Father Robbin's Borrowed Time Club.

Seated left to right: Mary Peake, Miss Eve; Laverne, Dr. Orvin Peake, Standing are Dr. William Russell Laverne, and his wife, Gertrude.

In 1878 George Nordenhold opened Oak Park's first bakery at 138 Lake (presently 1113 Lake). Mr. and Mrs. Nordenhold are seen in this 1884 photo standing together in front of their shop with baby George and the baker's two assistants. Nordenhold's delivery wagon guaranteed the timely arrival of fresh baked desserts and breads on his customers' dinner tables.

In 1872 H. W. Kaltenbach opened a hardware and tin shop in this brick two story building at 117-119 Lake Street near Harlem Ave. The elevated wooden sidewalks pictured here were designed to prevent pedestrians from sinking into a quagmire of mud as they did their shopping.

When the Cicero Township Board attempted to remedy the situation by grading and graveling Lake Street from Harlem to Oak Park Avenue, however, they met with violent opposition. A public meeting was held and people with mud holes in front of their homes and businesses denounced the improvement as unnecessary and extravagant, and as something that would destroy the rural simplicity of the village.

Frank Pebbles and his clerk Oscar Balch in front of Pebbles' Paint Store, which was opened in 1869 at 144 Lake Street near Harlem Ave. Balch later opened his own paint and decorating shop in the Masonic Block.

Before opening his shop Pebbles worked in the paint shop of the Chicago North Western Railroad in Harlem, where he practiced his art of portrait painting by painting the pictures of the president and other railroad officials on the headlights of the trains.

Pebbles later gained national recognition as a noted portrait artist. His full-length portrait of James W. Scoville hangs on the second floor landing of the present Oak Park Public Library.

The very first building erected on the northwest corner of Lake and Marion was a residence belonging to Albert Townsend, who occupied the east half of the house while his son Asia lived in the west portion. For many years it was known as the "old double house." The sprinkling cart shown in this photo kept the dust to a minimum on the unpaved streets, and was owned by George Townsend, a brother of Albert.

The Steiner Block was built on this site in 1886 and was used for a post office and several retail businesses. In 1928 R.E. Nicholas erected the present building for his hardware business. He later sold it to The Fair, a large Chicago department store. For a short time in the sixties it was owned by Montgomery Ward, and today is the site of Park Square.

O. W. Herrick had the distinction of being both Oak Park's first school principal and the first postmaster. In 1860 he was engaged to come from New York state to be principal of the new Oak Ridge Central school. He served in the post for five years, during which time he married Dora Kettlestrings, one of the daughters of Joseph Kettlestrings.

Herrick later became a traveling salesman for a publishing firm, but in 1871 opened a general store in this building at 208 Lake (now 1038) and began to compete with Steiner's grocery a block away.

Until 1871 Oak Ridge residents had received their mail at the Noyesville post office in Harlem. But when Herrick received the postmaster's commission from President Grant the post office was moved into this building. During the two years Herrick was postmaster he increased stamp sales to $10,000, which ranked the office as third class.

When Philandar Barclay took this photo in 1903 the building was being used by a Chinese laundry, one of four such establishments in the village at that time.

In 1855 Joseph Kettlestrings donated a lot at Forest and Lake for this nondescript white frame building that played not one, but several leading roles in Oak Park's history.

The building originally served as the village's first school from 1857 to 1859. As the enrollment continued to increase the lot across Lake Street (now 100 Forest Place) was purchased and the new Oak Ridge Central School was built in 1859.

It later became known as the "Mother of Churches," serving as the first church in this God-fearing community. At one time or another most of the major Protestant denominations held services in this building prior to constructing their own churches.

And finally, renamed Temperance Hall, it became a temple dedicated to sobriety by H. W. Austin, Sr. and his supporters, who were responsible for the 1872 Illinois Temperance Law which made Oak Park "dry" for more than 100 years.

The building, which was on property Kettlestrings had sold to Henry Austin, finally fell into disrepair and was razed in 1901.

DISTRICT 97 ELEMENTARY SCHOOL DISTRICT

Education in Oak Ridge was a rather haphazard affair before 1855 when Joseph Kettlestrings donated the land at the corner of Lake and Forest for a school. Prior to that classes had been conducted in homes, a situation the Kettlestringeses found so unsatisfactory that they left Oak Park and moved to Chicago from 1843 to 1854 so that their seven children could receive an education.

When Kettlestrings returned in 1854 the need for a permanent school was even more pressing. A small one-story frame school and meeting house was built on Kettlestrings' lot with the understanding that when a permanent school was erected the property would revert back to him. There were less than 20 pupils of all ages in the first class conducted in 1854 by A. D. Thomas.

In 1857 a regular district school was started in this overcrowded building with Miss Sarah Dewey as the teacher of 29 students of all ages. The establishment of this school was made possible by the organization of the congressional township into a school township.

Funding for this new school township came from the sale of a section of township land set aside for this purpose. The section was divided into 230 lots and sold for $100 an acre to provide school revenue. All the lots were sold but many were later foreclosed, and after all legal bills had been paid, a total of about $88,000 was realized for establishing the school district.

An addition was made to this school in 1858, but when it was apparent the enrollment would continue to climb, the lot across the street (today the site of 100 Forest Place) was purchased in March, 1859 for $1,100.

Work on the new school was pushed so quickly that the building was ready for occupancy in September, 1859. O.W. Herrick, who later married Dora Kettlestrings (a daughter of Joseph Kettlestrings), came from New York to be the principal of the new school.

Central School, as it came to be known, housed all 12 grades. The first high school graduating class of 1877 had three members: Herbert Whipple, Walter Gale, and James Herrick (son of O.W. Herrick and Dora Kettlestrings).

After graduating from college, James Herrick returned to Oak Park and taught Latin and Greek for two years to earn money for medical school. He later achieved world prominence as the first physician to recognize coronary thrombosis.

As the population of Oak Park increased, a separate high school was built in 1891 at the southwest corner of Lake and East Avenue on land purchased from James Scoville; and in 1899 a separate high school district was created. By 1880 two additions had been made to Central School. Ten more schools were built throughout Oak Park by 1921.

The class of 1867 standing in front of Oak Ridge School at Lake and Forest. All 12 grades were taught in this building until a separate high school was built at Lake and East Avenue in 1891.

This lot was purchased in 1859 for $1,100, from the proceeds of the sale of land set aside in the school township to provide school revenue. But while the taxpayers were willing to be taxed for the new Central School, they drew the line at paying for something as frivolous as a playground. Children went to school to learn, not to play!

James Scoville had more foresight and purchased the lot behind the school for $800. He held this property until the trustees recognized the need for a recreational area and then sold it to the school for what he had paid.

Scoville later must have felt great satisfaction watching the children erupt onto the playground after a day in the austere classroom to play baseball, pom-pom-pullaway, London Bridge, old cat, hopscotch and prisoner's base.

Knickers for boys and dresses for girls were the daily school attire at the turn of the century. Children were there to learn the three R's, which they did. It was a no frills education with emphasis on spelling, grammar, and penmanship, which these children are practicing at the black board under the watchful eye of their teacher.

An 1880 view of Central School after two additions had been added. The legend "Oak Ridge School District #1" was chiseled in stone on the north front of the original building. (The district number was changed from "1" to "97" in 1902 under a reorganization of county districts.)

The bell in the belfry rang not only to summon children to school but also for church, fires, and Fourth of July celebrations. When the building burned and was razed in 1924, both the marker and the bell were preserved.

The day of the McGuffey's readers had passed and this little girl is reading from a more "modern" textbook. The selections in these readers were intended to teach high moral standards in language suitable to the various grades.

In October, 1924 B.L. Dodge, Superintendents of Oak Park schools, laid the cornerstone of the new James Russell Lowell school on the site of the old Central School which had been partially destroyed by fire in 1924.

The needs of the growing community were continually changing. By 1958 many residences surrounding the school had been razed and the area had become primarily a business district.

But Lowell School's usefulness to the village was far from over. It provided temporary housing for several schools while their buildings were being renovated and also served as a library while the old Scoville Institute was razed and the present library built in 1964. It was also used as a Montessori School for several years. The last occupants of the building before it was demolished in 1972 were the elementary school board.

The history of Oak Park would be much different if a young man named James W. Scoville, walking from Chicago to Beloit College in Wisconsin, had not stopped to rest under a grand old oak atop a ridge that belonged to Joseph Kettlestrings.

After an impoverished childhood in New York, Scoville amassed a fortune through real estate and banking, and generously shared his wealth with his neighbors. He endowed Oak Park's first library, Scoville Institute, with a total of $115,000 for the building, furnishings and the lot at Lake Street and Grove Avenue. He also purchased the adjoining lot at Lake and Kenilworth for the First Congregational Church. In addition, Scoville could always be counted on to support any other worthy cultural or civic cause.

Scoville was president of the Prairie State Loan & Trust Bank, and together with several partners, purchased large tracts of land east of Oak Park Avenue which were then divided and subdivided into housing tracts.

After graduating from Beloit College, Scoville returned to New York where he married in 1853. He then returned to Oak Park with his family, where he purchased the lot at Lake Street and Oak Park Avenue from Joseph Kettlestrings. In 1857 he built his home on the spot where the War Memorial now stands.

In her book, "Little Old Oak Park", May Estelle Cook recalled Scoville as a delightful person, with friendly feeling toward people and a sense of humor that saved him from conceit and stuffiness.

"He had a genuine love of learning and of literature. Many mornings he would entertain the commuters at the station by reciting line after line of the 'Lady of the Lake' or other classics in a half-humorous way which showed his consciousness that his audience considered it queer for a businessman to know so much poetry."

Lake Street looking west around 1890, more closely resembling a bucolic country road than a busy thoroughfare. Scoville Institute and the First Congregational Church stand side by side, each representing not only the generosity of James Scoville, but the powerful religious, social and civic forces that bound the community together.

This photo shows the original church before lightning struck the 190 foot Gothic spire in 1916, destroying the entire church. It was rebuilt in 1918 with a shorter Norman tower on the west side.

By 1913 Scoville's home had been razed and plans for the 4.5 acre site were laid out by Jens Jensen, the internationally known landscape architect. On November 11, 1925 the granite and bronze monument honoring Oak Park's World War I heroes was unveiled in the presence of General C.G. Dawes, Vice President of the United States, and General John Pershing.

This fine example of Victorian architecture, with its propensity for "gingerbread" details, was built by James W. Scoville in 1857 on what is now the site of the World War I Memorial in Scoville Park.

Prior to his death in 1893 Scoville had retired to California because of his wife's failing health. For several years after his departure the home was used as a finishing school for girls.

In 1912 the newly created Park District of Oak Park paid $135,637 for both this property and another parcel owned by Scoville at Lake and Ridgeland, then known as the Old Cricket Grounds, but which today is Ridgeland Common.

Today's Oak Park Police Department bears little resemblance to the police protection offered to law-abiding villagers in the 1870's, when the first haphazard attempt was made to patrol Oak Park streets.

Fred Hacker, who was already employed to maintain the 65 coal-oil street lamps, became Oak Park's first policeman quite literally by chance. One day in 1878 he was sitting on his fence discussing the need for police service with two friends. Although money was scarce and the duties were hazardous, all three men were willing to take the job and agreed to draw lots.

Hacker drew the short end and so, for $45 a month paid by the Cicero Township Board, began patrolling village streets. "Marshall" Hacker, as he liked to be called, worked 12 hours a day and at midnight put out each of the street lights.

One of Hacker's duties was rescuing women and children from the pools of water that accumulated under the elevated board sidewalks on the undrained prairies. When he made an arrest he was forced to use a hand-car on the Chicago and Northwestern tracks to get the malefactor to the town hall in Austin, and since he supplied the motor power himself, he had to rope his man so he could not escape.

By 1892 Cicero Township had a combined police force of 16 men. This was considered inadequate to cover the 18 square miles of territory in the township. A committee appointed to make recommendations reported that the members of the force were "trustworthy but undisciplined".

No general orders were given and each man was allowed to decide just what his duties were and how he should perform them. Revolvers could not be counted on to fire and no records were kept as to arrests made. Also, the police did not know the street names and their locations since there was no uniformity in street names or numbers.

One of the major citizen complaints was that night patrol was completely inadequate, since each man on duty had to cover a beat of seven and a half miles. As a result, any enterprising burglar or thug could time the officer's patrol and, after he had passed, go about his nefarious business at his leisure.

In 1892 a patrol wagon and ambulance was purchased after one of the lieutenants collected $500 from various sources. The horse and wagon were kept across the street from the station at 213 Marian, a three story frame building the police shared with the fire department, until 1904 when both departments moved into the new municipal building at Lake and Euclid.

Shortly after the turn of the century, as more villagers traded in their horse and buggies for automobiles, the problem of safeguarding streets against "speeders" was added to the list of police duties.

Washington Blvd. had become a "drag strip" and so a patrolman was assigned to walk the street daily to protect pedestrians and property. He was equipped with a rope to stretch across the street to catch anyone who exceeded the legal speed limit of eight miles an hour.

The Oak Park Police force in 1904 in front of their new headquarters, the newly built municipal building at Lake and Euclid. The site is now occupied by the Prairies Court apartments but the cornerstone of this E.E. Roberts building has been preserved.

Third floor "loafing room" in the combined police and fire station, 213 Marion. This was one of the few all male bastions in the village where men came to enjoy camaraderie without any feminine distractions-except for these women shown in the theater bills and "spicy" pin ups prominently displayed on the walls.

Handlebar mustaches seemed to be an integral part of the uniform of the well dressed Oak Park police officer in the 1890's. Here three policemen pose with a cleanshaven young City Press reporter who had dropped by looking for a scoop.

Notice that the gas lights had already been changed to electric, and the "box" type telephone that stood on the floor in this Marion Street station.

Police marching down Oak Park Avenue in the 1903 Labor Day parade. The officer on the right (turning west onto North Blvd.) is Fred Hacker, the village's first police officer, who served 28 years on the force.

The Holley Block, 125-7 Lake Street, built by Nathan T. Holley around 1870, served the commercial as well as the intellectual and moral needs of the community. The storefront on the right was first used by the Oak Park Library Association, a privately subscribed library organized as a social club by a group of businessmen meeting at Pebbles' Paint Shop.

The men wanted to make it a smoker but smoking was taboo, so some scheme had to be devised to keep the club going. Someone suggested a library and the association was formed. In 1888 when Scoville Institute was completed, the association turned over its collection of 1,655 volumes to the new library and disbanded.

On the right is the entrance to the basement shop which was for many years the harness shop of Edward F. "Father" Robbins, founder of the Borrowed Time Club and a popular local figure. This photo can be dated either 1890 or 1891 because the small building across the alley housed the Oak Park News, a short-lived newspaper published by the Cordray Brothers during those two years.

The storefront was then rented by the Women's Christian Temperance Union, and became a center for temperance talks and lectures. The WCTU was a powerful force in the community since liquor had been banned in 1872. Berlin Grocery occupied the storefront of the right. The building was also known as the Hotel Leonard, an establishments which consisted of just a few rooms on the second floor.

"Father" Robbins in the harness shop he opened in the basement of the Holley building in 1872. The Borrowed Time Club, a group of elderly and revered citizens, was organized in this shop and met here for many years. Robbins died in 1910 at the age of 94.

OAK PARK FIRE DEPARTMENT

Oak Park's early settlers used their ingenuity to cope with many problems-save one. For many years fire control was an almost insoluble problem and fire remained the one disaster that could devastate a family or business. The frame buildings, kerosene lamps and dry grass all caused frequent fires and, with only primitive fire-fighting equipment, a fire usually went unchecked and resulted in complete destruction.

Fire protection in the 1870's consisted of a hand-drawn pumper that was often hauled to the fire by a milk wagon. Volunteer firemen, mostly tradesmen in the Lake and Marion street stores were called to fire duty by the ringing of the bell in the Central School belfry. At that point all business came to a halt and customers were left to fend for themselves as the shopkeepers rushed to duty.

The Reverend Francis Rowley, pastor of the First Baptist church, gave this sardonic description of early attempts at fire control: "Fire breaks out half a mile from our hose house. Someone must run through the streets shouting "fire" and carry the news to the hose house where, after much commotion, the doors are opened and all who are on hand seize the rope and our magnificent fire apparatus rolls grandly down the street and arrives in time, usually to cool off the ashes!"

In 1891 the Cicero Township Board passed an ordinance to create individual fire companies in the towns under its jurisdiction including Austin, Ridgeland and Oak Park. In commenting on the current system the Oak Park Reporter praised the efforts of the firemen but added, "The trouble is, it takes too long to give the alarm and too long to get the hose reels to the fire; also too long to notify the engineer at the water works to put on pressure."

Fire Company No. 1 was the Austin Company, the Ridgeland firehouse at Lake and Lombard was Company No. 2, and the Oak Park station at 213 Marion (which the firemen shared with the Oak Park police department) was No. 3. There was reportedly a good deal of rivalry between the three companies.

In 1895 Ridgeland stole a march on Oak Park by installing a system of fire alarm boxes and signals around the community that connected with both the engine house and the power house at Oak Park Avenue and North Boulevard.

As a result, when an alarm was given from a corner box, no time was wasted in dispatching the horse-drawn engine to the scene of the fire where water would immediately be available from a nearby hydrant that had already been primed by the engineer at the power plant, who had received the same signal.

In 1894 the Township Board finally appropriated $5,000 for horse drawn equipment to replace hand drawn carts. By 1906 the village, which was by then an independent governing body, bought its first chemical engine and hose wagon for $1,300.

In 1915 the fire department remodeled and motorized its old hook and ladder trucks. The old chemical tank was placed behind the driver's seat of a new Oldsmobile. The hook and ladder outfit was also attached to the car. The car could be used as a chemical engine when detached from the hook and ladder. It proved a success and marked the passing of the horse in the department.

This frame building served as headquarters for both the Oak Park Police and Fire Departments before both were moved to the new municipal building in 1904.

When the bell on the belfry rang, it was the signal for men to come running from their stores and businesses, putting on helmets and long white coats which they buttoned after jumping on the wagon. As many people as could stand on the running board of the wagon rode to the fire.

Volunteers of the Ridgeland Fire Company No. 2 responding to a call. There was great rivalry between the three neighboring fire companies. The Ridgeland Company proved itself one step ahead of its competitors in 1895 by installing a system of fire alarm boxes and signals connecting the community with the engine house and the power plant. A year later the other two companies followed suit with their own systems.

Oak Park Volunteer Fire Department No.3 poses on the Lombard side of the No. 2 fire house at Lombard and Lake. During the summer all the fire companies shared a common problem of constantly erupting prairie fires. Often one company was called upon to put out as many as eight fires in a single day.

Volunteer firemen M.M. McMahon and Ralph Smith in front of the No. 3 station, 213 Marion. Smith was also a City Press reporter and lived for a time in the sleeping quarters of the third floor "loafing room" where he was strategically placed for either a breaking story or an unexpected run on the fire wagon.

Henry W. Austin Sr., one of the first settlers of Oak Park and the founder of the village of Austin, was born in Onondaga County, New York in 1828. As a young man he came west without capital but represented several manufacturers of hardware. He was extremely successful and the profits from his business were invested in real estate in the Chicago area and in Kansas and Colorado.

Austin married Martha Voorhees in 1859, and the following year he purchased a six acre estate at Lake and Forest from Joseph Kettlestrings. The small frame building used for church services and other meetings was part of this parcel, and Austin allowed these meetings to continue.

In 1872 Austin, a member of the Illinois legislature, prepared and introduced the Illinois Temperance bill which became law on July 1, 1872. It was this law that kept Oak Park "dry" for more than 100 years. He renamed the building Temperance Hall and used it as the focal point for the temperance movement. Two Italian fresco artists were commissioned to paint a drop curtain for the hall, which depicted a beautiful woman pouring water into wine, the idea being temperance.

In 1866 Austin purchased and subdivided large parcels of land in what is now the Austin neighborhood of Chicago. He persuaded the United States Clock Manufacturing Company to locate there, and in recognition of this and other benefits which included a five acre park, it was decided to name the village in his honor.

This substantial home was built by Henry W. Austin, Sr. for his wife in 1860 on a six acre estate on the northwest corner of Lake and Forest. It was enclosed by a rustic wooden fence made from oaks growing near the Des Plaines River. This fence, which came to be a landmark for Oak Parkers, had to be replaced every seven or eight years.

The house originally faced Lake Street but in 1936 a Bank Holiday forced his son Henry W. Austin, Jr. to sell the choice frontage and move the house further back on the lot to 167 Forest.

In 1870 Henry W. Austin, Sr. built a private hall on his property which he made available to social and church groups for dances and parties. Villagers regularly used the grounds of the Austin home for other events, such as the gigantic torchlight parade held in 1872 anticipating Ulysses S. Grant's victory over Horace Greeley in the presidential election. From the grounds and porches of the Austin home Oak Parkers watched the senior Mr. Austin on horseback, garbed in a silver cape, leading the torchlight procession of the Tanners, hundreds of caped men who were supporters of Grant.

Henry W. Austin, Jr. died in 1947. Following the death of his wife Edna in 1964 the 104-year-old house became the property of the Park District. Austin had stipulated in his will that the house be leased to a not-for-profit village group. But since no willing group could be found at that time the house was demolished-a loss that is still lamented by members of the Historical Society of Oak Park and River Forest. The present Historical Society was not formed until 1968 and is presently in cramped quarters in the Farson-Mills house.

A saloon in Oak Park, a rare picture indeed! This picture was taken prior to 1872, the year Henry. W. Austin, Sr. agreed to purchase Oak Park's three saloons if Cicero Township would grant no more saloon licenses in Oak Park.

Austin bought the first two saloons but the owner of the third managed to keep it running. One day Austin called upon him and asked him how much he would take for his place, contents and all.

The man named and unreasonably high figure. Undaunted, Austin counted out the required sum and handed it over. Then saying, "This place is now mine," he immediately began pouring the liquor into the street.

The Farmer's Hotel and Tavern on the north side of Lake Street east of Marion, one of three Oak Park taverns purchased by Henry W. Austin for the purpose of closing them. Even though Oak Park was "dry", preaching against the evils of drink proved an uphill battle due to the presence of dozens of dram shops and gambling joints just blocks away on the west side of Harlem Avenue. According to several crusading clergymen Harlem Avenue was the dividing line between salvation and damnation.

To combat this peril the Women's Christian Temperance Union sponsored lectures and discussions. At a typical mother's meeting some 30 women heard a temperance talk and "gladly accepted the white ribbon with tears in their eyes saying they had suffered enough from the effects of liquor to hate it", according to a newspaper account.

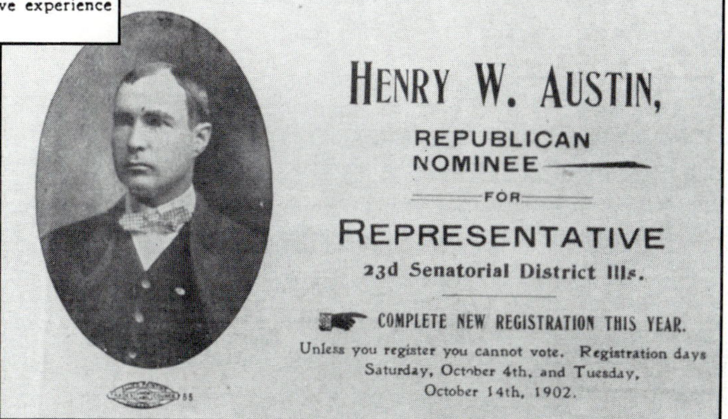

To the Republican Voters of the 23rd Senatorial District

A GRAVE PERIL CONFRONTS US

THE SALOON ELEMENT has openly declared its intention to secure the repeal of the Local Option Law at the next session of the Legislature of this State.

To that end it is carrying on a quiet, but thoro campaign to have nominated at the primary election next Saturday, August 8th, saloon candidates in almost every district in the state including the 23rd.

It seems to have been arranged that this district is to be represented in the next House by two Repulicans and one Democrat.

Next Saturday's primary is equivalent to an election, hence its importance.

Hon. Henry W. Austin has been our representative for some time, and his legislative experience is valuable to this district.

Headlines of a pre-election letter sent to voters by supporters of Henry Austin, Jr., who was being challenged in a Republican primary by "the saloon element that has openly declared its intention to secure the repeal of the Local Option Law at the next session of the legislature."

The letter was signed by some of the most prominent men in the community including John Farson, W.F. Van Bergen, James Goodwillie, E.E. Roberts, and Willis Herrick.

Henry W. Austin, Jr. followed his father's lead and also served in the Illinois legislature; he was elected in 1902 and served in both the House and Senate until 1922. During his tenure Austin supported all temperance legislation and defeated several attempts to repeal the temperance laws.

This prestigious home, at 917 Lake, was owned by C.E. Bolles, president of the Avenue State Bank until 1911. The site is now occupied by the Oak Park Post Office.

The home of E.O. Gale, built in 1867 on the northwest corner of Lake and Kenilworth in the Gothic Revival style. Gale was a second generation Oak Parker. His father, Abram Gale, emigrated from England and arrived in Chicago in 1835, the same year the federal government held the first public sale of land between Chicago and Ottawa. Gale bought a 320 acre tract north of what is now North Avenue, which he subdivided into a town many years later and gave the name Galewood.

CHAPTER II

GROWTH
AND
DEVELOPMENT

1872-1902

During the "gay nineties" Oak Park was a setting straight out of a Booth Tarkington novel. Propriety, provincialism, and prudery were the prevailing virtues. People placed a high value on work, family life, well-defined social amenities, conservative politics, regular church attendance and simple, family-oriented recreation.

The majority of Oak Parkers were staunch Republicans and the presence of a Democrat was so rare that it was considered newsworthy. After an 1894 voter registration drive the Oak Park Reporter commented that "30 new voters were registered here Tuesday. Two of the the gentlemen are said to be of the Democratic persuasion. If this is so, Sam Carmen will have some company and will no longer be compelled to travel alone, so far as congenial political society is concerned." The Republicans of Oak Park met regularly at Hoard's Hall but the Democratic party in Oak Park wasn't organized until 1939.

Politics weren't the only things that interested villagers who, without the distraction of television to keep them at home, prided themselves on the number of clubs in which they could claim membership.

Many of these groups met in Scoville Institute which served as a cultural and civic center as well as a library. The Romanesque building erected in 1888 at Lake Street and Grove (on the site of the present library) was the gift of James W. Scoville, who donated more than $115,000 to cover the cost of the lot, building and an endowment.

There was a club in Oak Park for everyone, whatever their age and whatever their interests. Only the most reclusive citizen could be counted on to be "at home" more than a few nights a week.

But however festive the soiree, dance, or party, after the Temperance Law was passed in 1872 it was unaccompanied by so much as a drop of liquor. The Women's Christian Temperance Union maintained a busy schedule of temperance lectures and socials and was a force to be reckoned with in the community, as backsliders and would-be imbibers found to their chagrin.

The Chicago Fire was the catalyst for a population explosion in the 1870's. Oak Park's population skyrocketed from approximately 500 in 1871, the year of the fire, to 9,889 in 1902 when Oak Park severed its ties with Cicero Township and was incorporated as a self-governing municipality.

William Halley, peppery editor of the Oak Park Vindicator, summarized some of the reasons prospective homeowners chose Oak Park:

"Oak Park is located eight miles west of the Chicago River with an abundant elevation. It is a bower of beauty. It is the home of luxury and refinement. Here education flourishes and religion and temperance triumph. There is no place for anything that savors of discord or disorder. Saloons are excluded. Animals are not allowed to roam and a hog or cow is never seen on the street. The streets are always cleanly kept. One feels relaxation and comfort within its borders and along its shaded walks. Gaily dressed children romp and the air is vocal with the music of their sweet voices. Churches, schools and society halls meet the eye at every turn."

To meet the demand for new housing the remaining parcels of Joseph Kettlestring's original section of land in Kettles-tring's Grove, as well as other land east of Oak Park Avenue and south of the North Western tracks, was divided and subdivided for tract housing by developers such as Milton Niles, Josiah Lombard, James Scoville, O.W. Herrick, and William Ogden.

The architecture of the majority of homes built during this period was variations of the popular Queen Anne style. In 1889, however, a brash 22-year-old architect named Frank Lloyd Wright built an innovative new shingle style home for his family on the prairie north of Lake Street on Chicago Avenue.

This uncomplicated house, with roof and walls that were covered with cedar shingles and accented by leaded diamond shaped window panes, was the precursor of Wright's Prairie Style of architecture that would revolutionize the nature of the American home in the following years.

As quickly as the need for housing was satisfied, the lack of a sufficient number of schools became apparent. In 1872 Central School, a single building at Lake and Forest built in 1859 and enlarged three times, served as both a high school and an elementary school. By 1902 a separate high school district had been created and, in addition to Central School (or Lowell School as it came to be called), there were six new grammar schools built to serve the young families purchasing these large homes.

During the 1870s the God-fearing citizens of Oak Park built so many churches that the community came to be known as "Saint's Rest." By 1880 every major Protestant denomination was represented by a church and most had met at one time or another during their formative years at Temperance Hall.

It is interesting to note that many of Oak Park's first churches were destroyed by fire; their soaring Gothic spires made them quite literally lightning rods during electrical storms. Most churches, like the First Congregational Church (now First United Church of Oak Park), chose to rebuild with more solid Norman towers which made them less susceptible to being struck by lightning.

Although the social and moral tone of Oak Park remained essentially unchanged during this period, it was also a time of great political upheaval. At the turn of the century most citizens were chafing under the political yoke of the Cicero Township Board, which since 1857 had governed Oak Park, Austin, Ridgeland, Berwyn and other small communities in Cook County that had not been incorporated into Chicago in 1837.

As early as 1880 a separate government for Oak Park had been discussed but no law existed under which such an organization could be set up. Finally, in 1891 the Illinois assembly passed an act for the separation of incorporated towns which stated that none of the separate towns could vote themselves out of the township, but the entire township had to vote on the question.

Unfortunately, there was a good deal of friction between the communities and jealousy of Oak Park's greater share of wealth and influence. As a result of this rancor, Oak Park's first attempt to break away from Cicero Township in an 1895 election was defeated by votes coming out of the Austin community.

The opposition by Austin to the division of Cicero Township embittered Oak Park voters, who returned the favor and mustered a vote large enough to have Austin annexed by Chicago even though most Austinites opposed the annexation. At the same time Oak Park citizens voted themselves out of Cicero Township.

Austin residents challenged the vote in court but the Supreme Court upheld the annexation, and so Austin reluctantly became part of Chicago. In the same decision, however, the Supreme Court negated the Act of 1891 and ruled no law existed under which separate municipalities could be established - leaving Oak Park at square one as an unwilling chattel of Cicero Township.

By now, however, there was no turning back. Oak Parkers were determined to end their domination by Cicero Township and to form a self-governing municipality. A committee was appointed in 1899 to draw up an amendment to the Cities and Villages Act that would permit separation.

The law was passed by the Illinois legislature and went into effect on July 1, 1901. Oak Park residents lost no time in organizing their next move under this new law. An election was held on November 5, 1901 and the proposition was carried by a large majority.

In December of that year the first slate of eight officials, including a president, six trustees, and a village clerk, were elected. The first formal session of the new Board was held on January 2, 1902 in Scoville Institute. Subsequent meetings were held at the library and at other locations in the village until completion of the new Municipal Building at Lake Street and Euclid in 1904.

These school boys in knickers might be trudging up Oak Park Avenue to Chicago Avenue on their way to Holmes School. Around the turn of the century Oak Park Avenue was lined with imposing Victorian homes from Lake Street to Chicago Avenue, including the one at 439 N. Oak Park in which Ernest Hemingway was born in 1899. Many of these homes were demolished in the 1920s to make way for large apartment buildings.

A view from North Blvd. looking north on Oak Park Avenue in the early 1890s. The row of buildings on the left, which were the first businesses on Oak Park Avenue, are still standing today. (The first block south of South Blvd. on Oak Park Avenue was filled with handsome homes until after the turn of the century when stores began to replace them.)

In 1888 Mr. Goelitz, the plumber, built the double two-story brick building on the northwest corner of Oak Park Avenue and North Blvd., which housed his shop as well as Nissen and Puchner's grocery and meat market.

Notice both the fire hydrant and the electric light pole on the west side of the street. The Cicero Water, Gas, and Electric Light Company plant, which was located across the street from these buildings on the present site of Avenue Bank, provided the communities in Cicero Township with both electricity for street lighting and sufficient water pressure for these hydrants to enable fire fighters to successfully contain a fire. A signal from a neighborhood fire alarm box that was connected to both the fire station and the water plant alerted the engineer to increase water pressure in the hydrants nearest to the fire.

The gradual incline or "ridge" past Lake Street which gave Oak Park its original name of Oak Ridge is very evident in this picture.

James Carter, iceman and village bon vivant, stopping on his route at Washington Blvd. and Wesley. According to an item in the Oak Park Reporter, Carter, whose ice plant was located on South Blvd., got out his sleigh one night and gave 15 telephone operators an evening of sleighing.

"They were entertained at the home of Margaret Glynn with fire chief Carlisle acting as chaperone. Chris Hofner offered free use of Kenilworth Hall for their dance in April. Chris says he is a great admirer of the fair 'hello girls' and is just as good a fellow as Jim Carter. But Jim is the ice man and unmarried, too, while Chris is neither."

Before the turn of the century, Sam Postlewait opened his first funeral parlor in Oak Park at 107 Marion. In 1902 when Charles B. Scoville (the son of James Scoville) built the Scoville Building on the southeast corner of Lake and Oak Park Avenues, Postlewait occupied the space shown in this photo, which is now used by Haagen Daz Ice Cream, at 134 N. Oak Park Avenue.

In 1925 Postlewait moved to the building at 720 Lake Street that had been erected specifically for the funeral home by the Scoville estate, with a 25 year lease. When this lease ran out in 1950, still another move was made to the present facility at 523 Lake Street.

The Cicero Water, Gas and Electric Light Company was a publicly owned company which supplied basic utilities to village homes. This facility at Oak Park Avenues and North Blvd., on the site of Avenue Bank, had its beginnings in 1878 when James Scoville built a reservoir over an existing pond on this property for private use.

In 1885 Scoville made a private contract with owners of property on north Oak Park Avenue to enlarge his reservoir and extend service to them. Two years later, the water plant and pumping station became a publicly owned corporation supplying water to homes and hydrants throughout the village, using water pumped from nine artesian wells each 2,175 feet deep. The company was reorganized in 1899 with an increased capital stock and its name was changed to the Chicago Suburban Water and Light Company.

By 1905 the combination of a deteriorating plant and a typhoid scare prompted calls for the village to build its own municipal water works. In 1908 bonds were issued and the first water main laid. The village water system merged with the Chicago water supply in 1912 when this connection was turned at North Blvd. and Euclid. This completed the transfer of the old pipe system to municipal ownership and allowed water from Lake Michigan to flow into village taps.

In 1880 Charles D. Drechsler, a member of a prominent Oak Park family, opened the village's first mortuary on Lake Street. In 1898 he built Oak Park's first "skyscraper," this three-story building at 135 Lake Street (now 1116 Lake) which houses Katie's Country Candies today.

It was the only steel reinforced building west of the loop and was used as both a funeral parlor and headquarters for another Drechsler enterprise, a moving and storage company. After World War I Drechsler also operated an agency on this site for the short-lived Franklin auto.

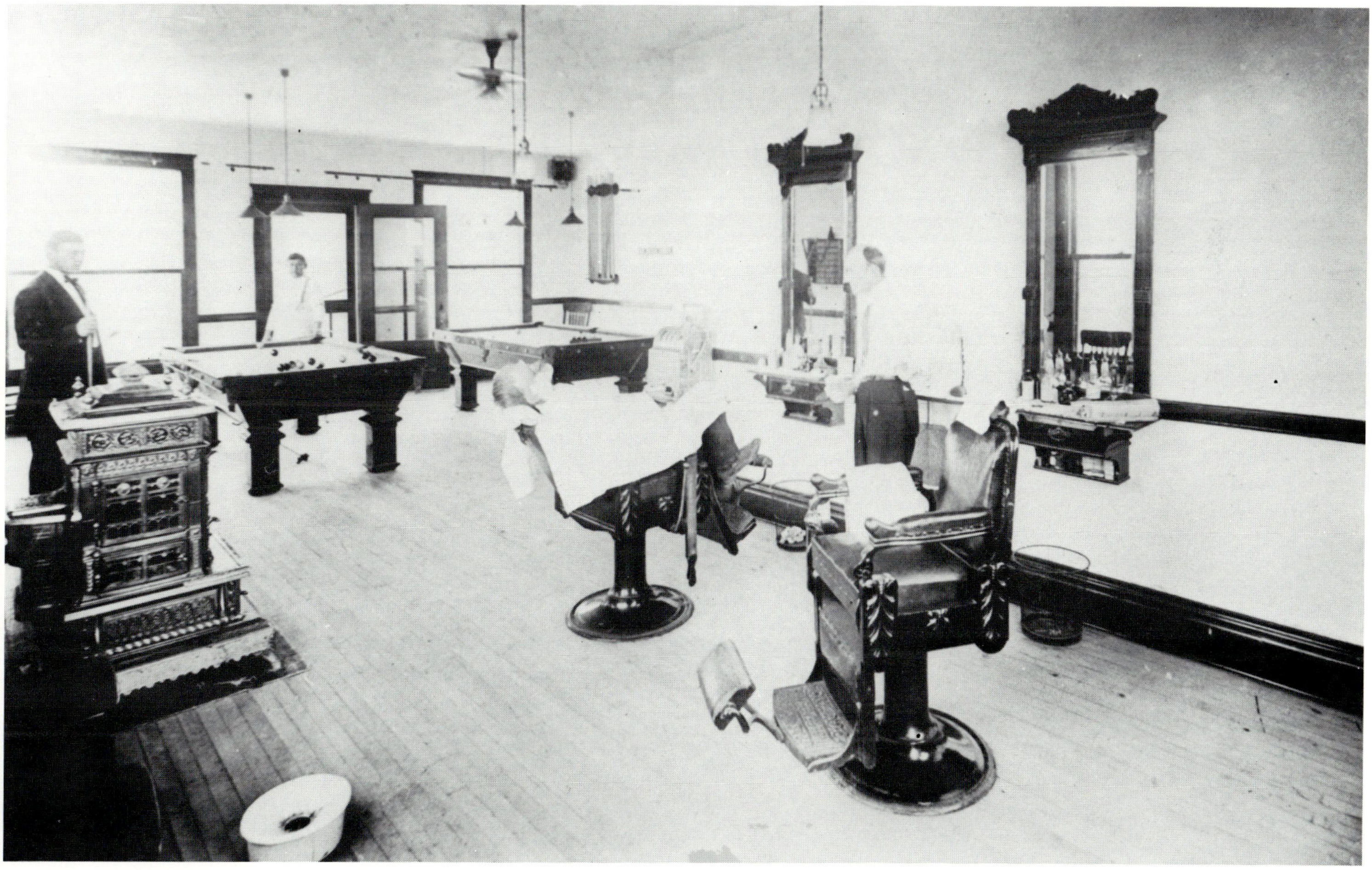

An unidentified barber shop, possibly belonging to August Miller who is known to have opened the first barber shop. His brother, Peter, operated the village's first butcher shop on Lake Street and did his own slaughtering on the premises.

Although the shop is short on the ambiance found in many barber shops today, it had all the amenities needed at the time, including a spittoon and pool tables.

Although they were few in number, there were some professional women in Oak Park before the turn of the century. Dr. Emily Huff, shown here leading a horse from her barn on Chicago Avenue between Forest and Marion, was the physician for the Frank Lloyd Wright family during the 1890s and early 1900s.

Another professional woman was the Reverend Augusta Chapin, Congregational minister and pastor of Unity Church of Oak Park.

Post Office Block at 105 Marion

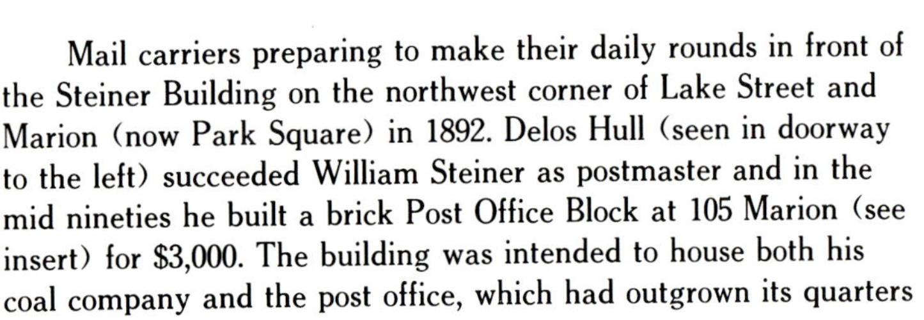

Mail carriers preparing to make their daily rounds in front of the Steiner Building on the northwest corner of Lake Street and Marion (now Park Square) in 1892. Delos Hull (seen in doorway to the left) succeeded William Steiner as postmaster and in the mid nineties he built a brick Post Office Block at 105 Marion (see insert) for $3,000. The building was intended to house both his coal company and the post office, which had outgrown its quarters in the Steiner Building.

At this time Oak Park, River Forest, and Forest Park had combined into one postal district and mail was placed and collected by carriers for the first time. Mail boxes were also placed throughout the village in the hope that fewer letters would be carried about in the city all day and brought home again by forgetful husbands, fathers, and brothers.

Elijah Hoard in the sitting room of his home on Marion Street and Westgate (called Hoard's alley), just half a block from his place of business. In addition to his real estate interests, Hoard also served as Justice of the Peace and as a trustee for Cicero Township. he was active in Father Robbins' Borrowed Time Club and died in 1908 at the age of 95.

Marion Street looking south from Lake Street. Lovett's Drug Store is on the left and Hoard's Hall on the right. Marion (spelled today with an "o" instead of an "a") was named after Marian Niles, daughter of Milton Niles, a prominent developer. It is one of the oldest streets in the village and is part of the Niles subdivision.

As early settlers laid out new streets they generally named them after their offspring. (For example, all of the street surrounding Kettlestring's Grove were named for Kettlestrings' children: Oak Park Avenue was Walter Street and Kenilworth was named for Willis.)

Later all these family names were changed - with the exception of Marion. Until 1880 Marion only ran from the North Western tracks to Lake Street. Later it was cut through to Chicago Avenue.

Hoard's Block, on the southwest corner of Lake Street and Marion, was built in 1876 by Elijah Hoard, a developer who owned considerable property in the village. The first floor was occupied by stores while the second floor was used as a public hall where villagers danced during the week and prayed on Sunday.

Schneider's Grocery on the northeast corner of Lake and Marion in the 1880s, on the present site of First Chicago Bank of Oak Park. This picture details three widely different forms of transportation: the horse and carriage favored by a customer; the delivery wagon used by the grocery and the diminutive goat cart popular with the children.

GROCERIE

SCOVILLE INSTITUTE - OAK PARK PUBLIC LIBRARY

The Oak Park Public Library that today utilizes the latest in computer technology in it day-to-day operations is a far different facility than the massive stone Scoville Institute funded by James Scoville before the turn of the century.

Today's Oak Park Library has 240,000 cataloged volumes and offers patrons a wide variety of technologically advanced services including document indexing, tapes, videocassettes, compact discs and computerized check-out.

In contrast, Scoville Institute (as the village's first library was called), had only a few thousand volumes when it was built in 1888, but its prominent position as a social, cultural and civic center during the Gay Nineties and beyond more than made up for its original dearth of books.

In 1883 James Scoville announced he would donate $75,000 for the formation of a cultural and civic center that would be financed by dues-paying members. Villagers were also asked to subscribe to a library fund which would be used to purchase books.

A committee of fourteen prominent men was named to oversee the project. Articles of incorporation were written and Norman Patton's design for a Romanesque building of Bedford stone was accepted. The cornerstone was laid on September 4, 1886 and by the time the building was dedicated in October, 1888 Scoville's gift for the building, lot and endowment totaled $115,000.

The Institute was an immediate success. By 1889 more than 1,000 library cards had been issued and throughout the Gay Nineties it served as the center for much of Oak Park's social life. On any given day villager could choose a book on the first floor, attend a lecture, meeting, or other cultural activity on the second floor, and even work out at the Institute's gymnasium on the third floor. (The gym was soon abandoned after complaints that it was too noisy.)

It was soon apparent, however, that Scoville Institute's endowment fund was insufficient to keep pace with increased demands, and by the terms of Scoville's gift, no charge could be made for the use of the books or building. The town was growing and the trustees felt that a building which opened its doors to all should not be supported by a few. In 1902 the village had broken from Cicero Township and formed an independent unit of government. The following year the Institute received public funds from this government when villagers agreed in a referendum to submit to a tax for support of a public library.

The referendum provided for a Library Board to be elected and two mills out of every dollar of state taxes were to be used for support of the library. Although Scoville Institute provided villagers with a library before the turn of the century, it has only been since 1903 that the library has been tax supported.

Many villagers are unaware that from 1903 until 1961 when it was decided to demolish Scoville Institute and build a new library, there were actually two library boards. The Scoville Board held actual title to the building and land but its members had no voice in policy-making decisions, while members of the elected library board were responsible for all library policy.

In 1961 the Scoville Board dissolved itself and turned its assets over to the elected library board with the stipulation that the words "Scoville Institute" be carved in stone on the lintel above the main entrance of the new library. They felt it was only fitting to perpetuate the name of James Scoville and the library that would not have existed without his generous gift of both money and land.

By 1964 the new Oak Park Public Library was completed on the site of Scoville Institute. A second story addition was completed in 1977.

Scoville Institute, the gift of James Scoville to the people of Oak Park. Built in 1888, the Romanesque building served as a cultural and civic center for the community as well as a library.

Cornerstone Laying ceremonies in 1886. Scoville's home is in the background.

The reference room in Scoville Institute during the 1950s, filled to capacity. To meet the growing demand for services in a building that was becoming inefficient and obsolete by modern standards, the Library Board began to plan for a larger and more modern facility. Scoville Institute was razed in 1964 and today's Oak Park Public Library was built on the site.

A young reader confers with the librarian on his choice of books. Scoville Institute was the first library in Illinois to have a children's room and a children's librarian.

James Scoville looks down benevolently at a display of children's books. A voracious reader himself, Scoville would have approved of the sentiment on the poster next to his portrait: "What a child thinks is in great measure determined by the books he reads."

Scoville's portrait was hung in several different locations in Scoville Institute through the years. Today the painting by Frank Pebbles, a nationally recognized portrait artist who also owned a paint and decorating business in Oak Park, hangs on the second floor landing of the Oak Park Public Library.

The reading habit was nurtured early as shown in this photo of a kindergarten class held at Scoville Institute in the early 1900s. Each child decorously faces the camera, book in hand.

Miss Moore's library training class at Scoville Institute around 1907. The duties of these young ladies were far less complicated than those of today's Oak Park librarians. No matter how obtuse the question they never fail to point the person in the right direction.

In contrast, this young man during the fifties assumes a more casual pose while engrossed in a book that has captured his fancy, oblivious of his surroundings and the fact that the librarian is about to remind him that chairs, not tables, are used for sitting.

Scoville Institute's check out desk during the 1940s when everything was still done by hand, before the arrival of the computer's magic wand that "beeps" books out.

Notice the library's phone number on the poster. Numbers had not yet replaced letters and "383" was still "Euclid."

The Oak Park Public Library was completed in 1964 and the second story addition was added in 1977. The sculpture in front of the building, "Unity and Growth" by Carole Harrison, was the winning entry in a competition sponsored by the Village Art Fair, which purchased the sculpture and donated it to the library.

When this building was erected in 1891 at the southeast corner of Prairie (now Kenilworth) and South Blvd., it was known as the Prairie Cycling Club and was a gathering place for cyclists during the Gay Nineties.

As the popularity of cycling began to wane, members were absorbed into the Oak Park Club. When the name Prairie was changed to Kenilworth, the building became known as Kenilworth Hall.

In 1903 when this photo was taken the Oak Park Machine Company was in the basement. It was also here a few years later that the first "Silent Knight Motor" invented by a villager, C.Y. Knight, was built.

The building was later the home of the Oak Parker and the Oak Leaves. During World War II, the third floor was used as an armory.

A group of young cycling enthusiasts stopping to rest after a strenuous ride. Notice the differences in bicycles. The conventional two-wheeled "safety" bike resting on the ground must have been the easier to ride, but the "bonebreaker" or high wheel bicycle resting against the tree was the more popular during the 1880s.

While all the village's young people enjoyed an active social life, it was always pursued in groups. Girls never went to parties or any other gathering without a chaperone, either a friend or an older woman.

The Nineteenth Century Women's Club, still the largest women's club in Oak Park, was founded in 1890 by a group of 30 women for the purpose of studying the events and accomplishments of the first half of the nineteenth century. The women met in several locations including Scoville Institute. By 1916 the Club had outgrown every hall in town and a fund raising drive resulted in the purchase of a lot at Grove and Ontario.

World War I delayed plans for the new club, however, and by the end of the war the original lot was deemed too small. A lot at Forest and Ontario was purchased in 1924 and a successful drive raised the $60,000 needed to construct the present building at 178 Forest, which opened in 1928.

The Warrington Opera House was built in 1902 on the southeast corner of South Blvd. and Marion. The opening was a gala event with 40 members of Theodore Thomas' Chicago Symphony Orchestra furnishing the music, along with a chorus of 200 singers from Oak Park and River Forest.

"Everything under the sun" was tried here and for several years the theater prospered, but eventually it came to be used only for plays given by local talent and traveling stock companies. In 1930 the building was remodeled for various purposes including moving pictures. Today it is Marlac House, a banquet facility.

Oak Park's first orchestra, photographed in 1886. The headquarters for the group at this time was on the third floor of the Hansen building, 101-3 Lake Street. Front row left to right (seated): Hugo Walthers, Edwin Walthers, Vern Brado, and Victor Timme. Standing: Frank Kohn, Morris Czmock, Ed Czmock, and Frank Timme.

OAK PARK CHURCHES TO 1910

Once the God-fearing settlers of Oak Ridge had built their homes in Kettlestrings Grove, their next priority was to organize and establish churches that would imbue their children with the faith of their forefathers.

Although Joseph Kettlestrings was one of the founding fathers of the First Methodist Church in Oak Ridge, he generously provided a place for other denominations to meet in the small frame building at Forest and Lake. That building was originally used as the village's first school from 1857 to 1859, but came to be known as the "Mother of Churches" because of its frequent use as a house of worship.

In 1860 Henry W. Austin, Sr. purchased a six acre tract of land fronting on Lake Street from Joseph Kettlestrings. The property, which was enclosed by a rustic wooden fence, included the "Mother of Churches."

Austin continued to allow the building to be used for religious services but in 1872 it also became the focal point of the temperance movement. Austin renamed the building Temperance Hall and commissioned two Italian fresco artists to paint the drop curtain which hung at one end of the hall. The scene depicted a beautiful maiden pouring water into wine, the idea being temperance.

By 1910 every major Protestant denomination, as well as one Catholic parish, was represented by a church and most had met at one time or another in Temperance Hall. In fact, the increase in the number of churches was so rapid that the suburb was often referred to as "Saint's Rest."

According to a much-quoted story, two teamsters were driving a wagon of goods from the city to Oak Ridge. When the driver asked his companion how he should know when he was in Oak Ridge, the man replied, "When you get where the saloons stop and the churches begin, you will know that you are there."

The first sermon in Oak Ridge was given in 1856 by a Methodist preacher, James Viall. It was delivered in Temperance Hall to a congregation that included Joseph Kettlestrings. In 1873 Kettlestrings donated land on the northeast corner of Lake Street and Forest as the site of the First Methodist Church.

In 1888 the church was enlarged but in 1923 the entire structure was destroyed by fire. Plans were made at once to rebuild at the corner of Oak Park Avenue and Superior Street. The present Gothic church at 324 N. Oak Park Avenue was completed in 1925.

Presbyterian services were first conducted in Oak Park as early as 1861, but it was not until 1883 that a group of villagers including Dr. Orin Peake organized the First Presbyterian Church. A small frame church was dedicated in 1886 at what is now 931 Lake Street, and in 1901 this building was replaced by a stone and brick church on the same site.

In 1975 the congregation of the First Presbyterian Church merged with the First Congregational Church at 848 Lake Street to form the First United Church of Oak Park. This new church uses the Congregational facilities.

In 1979 the former Presbyterian church building was purchased by Calvary Memorial Church, which had been renting the facilities since the loss of their own church in a 1975 fire.

Congregationalists can rightly claim to be the first established religion to hold services in Oak Park. In 1860 a group of families formed the Union Ecclesiastical Society of Oak Ridge and began holding non-sectarian services in Temperance Hall, using doctrine commonly known as Congregational. The Society then formed a Union Church call Oak Ridge Church of Harlem in 1863. In 1871 this Church became the First Congregational Church, a move that caused some members to break with the Church.

James Scoville donated a lot at Kenilworth and Lake Street for the building of a new Congregational Church. Total cost for this 1873 Gothic building ornamented with stained glass and a 190 foot spire was $47,100. The building was destroyed by fire in 1916 but was rebuilt in 1918 on the same site.

Today the former Congregational Church is known as the First United Church of Oak Park since merging with the First Presbyterian Church in 1975.

The First Baptist Church was organized in Oak Park in 1873 in the home of J.W. Middleton. The small congregation met at Temperance Hall until 1883 when their church on the southeast corner of Wisconsin and Pleasant was completed. In 1918 they purchased land at Oak Park Avenue and Ontario where they built their present church.

St. Edmunds, the first of four Catholic parishes in Oak Park, was established in 1907. Prior to that Catholics had been worshiping at St. Luke's in River Forest. A site was bought at the northeast corner of Oak Park Avenue and Pleasant, and the Gothic church and rectory were completed in 1910. The school, across Pleasant Street and facing Oak Park Avenue, was completed in 1917. It is modeled after the Hall of Justice in Rouen, France.

Unity Church of Oak Park, the predecessor of Frank Lloyd Wright's famed Unity Temple, was a simple Gothic church built in 1872 on Wisconsin Avenue near Pleasant. The congregation, which consisted of many of the village's most prominent citizens, had been a part of the Oak Ridge Church of Harlem. When that church moved to join the Congregational fold, members with more liberal views broke away to form their own church.

This small society, which consisted of both Unitarians and Universalists, combined their creeds in a statement acceptable to both and met at Temperance Hall until their church was completed. In 1905 the church spire was struck by lightning and the building was a total loss.

Frank Lloyd Wright, a young architect who was a member of the congregation, was given the commission to design a new building in a more central location at Kenilworth and Lake Street.

Working with a budget of only $45,000 Wright created an innovative design that included the dignity appropriate to a church but eliminated the expense of a soaring roof and spire. Today Unity Temple is considered one of the most important examples of Wright's Prairie School architectural style. It is a National Historic Landmark and is listed on the National Register of Historic Places.

Prior to 1879 Episcopalians in Oak Park had been worshiping at Christ Church in River Forest, but in that year they withdrew from the River Forest congregation and held services in Hoard's Hall until 1883 when their first church at Forest and Ontario was dedicated.

In 1901 the cornerstone was laid for the present Gothic church at 924 Lake Street. By 1905 the main church was completed, with the exception of the tower which was not finished until 1922.

The first Evangelical Lutheran Church in Oak Park, called Emmanuel Congregation, was established in 1864 when a small group of German-speaking settler began holding services in Temperance Hall. In 1867 this first building was erected on Ontario near Marion, and it was rebuilt in 1896. The present church, completed in 1916 on the northwest corner of Ontario and Marion, is currently used by St. John's United Methodist Church.

An 1896 portrait of the handsome Queen Anne home owned by the Edwin T. Johnson family at 329 S. Home (now 327). The presence of various family members enjoying their home makes this an especially interesting picture. The carriage drawn up to the front of the house is possibly waiting to take the ladies on the porch shopping. The boy on the Shetland pony is one of the few children in the village lucky enough to own such a pet. The other child seems to prefer his bicycle, while his siblings on the stoop are perhaps awaiting their turn on the pony.

Three years later and a few blocks north of the Johnson family, the Frank Lloyd Wright family poses in front of their new shingle style home on Chicago Avenue, which was a variation of the Queen Anne style home.

In 1889 Frank Lloyd Wright, a 22-year-old maverick architect, married Catherine Tobin and built this home for her. The roof and walls were covered with cedar shingles which were complimented by leaded paned windows. There were wide doorways on the first floor enabling the family to look from one room into others. And, rather than each room being a little box as in most Queen Anne homes, each room borrowed space from the adjoining rooms and space seemed to flow through the house.

It was in this home, and in the attached studio built in 1898, that Wright developed his distinctive Prairie Style of architecture. The free-flowing spaces of this style, the interweaving of interior and exterior, ground-hugging horizontals marked by long bands of windows, and the use of natural materials all revolutionized the nature of the American home.

This handsome 3 story brick building which is standing to-day was built in 1897 at Marian and Westgate by Wright Elsom. The first tenants in the Elsom Block included Milton Niles who had purchased this entire section from Joseph Kettlestrings and subdivided it and James S. Barclay, father of village chronicler Philander Barclay. Barclay's drug store called the Golden Lion became a gathering place where villagers congregated to exchange gossip.

Interior view of James Barclay's drug store, which had one of the first telephones in the village. Young Philander was called upon to deliver messages as they were received and, as a result, he probably knew more about the lives of his neighbors than anyone else.

"My father's drug store was the gossiping center of the whole town," he said. "I used to listen to the jovial tales and I thought nobody ever thinks about saving the past until the past is gone. Someday they'll be early history."

To ensure the past would never be erased, "Bicycle Barclay" (as he came to be called) slung his bulky black camera across his shoulder and pedaled through the village taking over 600 pictures of village life. More important, he painstakingly identified every person and building in each picture as well as the location.

Today Barclay's collection is priceless because it not only makes it possible to pictorially recreate the village street by street, but also because his photographs and text provide a chronicle of a leisurely and gracious way of life that no longer exists.

Philander W. Barclay had no business sense and the bicycle repair shop was his only successful business venture. When the cycling craze died he found himself without income. For the rest of his life Barclay never held a regular job and spent what little money he had on photographic equipment. In his later years he lived with his sister, who shared her teacher's pension with him; after her death he relied on the charity of friends. Barclay died alone and penniless on July 7, 1940.

All his life Barclay's interests and actions were seemingly at odds with one another. Nothing interested him more than village affairs and people. He talked to hundreds and knew thousands of Oak Parkers by name yet had no intimate friends and in the half century he lived in Oak Park he never joined any group, society, club or church. He seemed content to hover on the periphery of village life, recording but never participating.

After his parents died within weeks of each other in 1902, Philander Barclay opened this bicycle sales and repair shop. He never borrowed money and was not a believer in credit. Children whose fathers were among the wealthiest couldn't get their bicycles out of Barclay's shop until they had paid for their repairs. He would repair a bicycle without charge, however, if he considered the owner unable to afford the repairs.

A view of the "old cricket grounds" at Ridgeland and Lake which was used as an athletic field for baseball, cricket, and football in the 1890s. In 1912 commissioners from the newly formed Park District purchased this site from Charles B. Scoville, son of James Scoville, for use as a park.

Soon after the purchase of this lot now known as Ridgeland Common, citizens began a campaign to raise money and persuaded the Park Commissioners to purchase the land directly west of it.

Around $3,000 was raised, and the Park District paid the balance of $18,000 to buy the block bounded by Lake, North Blvd., Elmwood and Scoville. This additional ground gave Ridgeland Common a total area of 9.1 acres. In 1929 the Park District erected a memorial boulder to Spanish American War veterans on this site.

The Spanish American War in 1898 was fought entirely by volunteers such as these men from Company D, First Regiment, Illinois National Guard. This photo was taken in 1898 in Jacksonville, Florida. The Oak Park "boys" are, left to right: E.D. Bicknell, Edwin Schneider, Phillip Van Vlack, George Haven, and Ralph Sherman; seated; Dan Stone. Stone and Haven later died in service.

An Oak Park baseball team of 1890. Organized teams such as this used the baseball grounds at Madison and Clinton.

Villagers enjoyed fresh produce supplied by Gus Cutsuvites, who opened this fruit stand on the west side of Marion south of Lake about 1896. Like all other Oak Park shops, this stand, which folded into a compact box when not is use, was closed on Sunday.

The Gotsch building at the northeast corner of Chicago Avenue and Marion was one of only a handful of business establishments on Chicago Avenue in the 1890s. That area did not become a business center of any significance until the 1920s.

This building housed the E. J. Gotsch grocery and market and was most likely patronized by the Frank Lloyd Wright family. It is now owned by H.L. Meilahn and is occupied by Granny's Deli.

The Niles Block, built in 1891 by developer Milton Niles on the southwest corner of South Blvd. and Marion, across the street from the Warrington Theater, is currently being restored by a modern developer.

The building housed a number of retail businesses including Owens Brothers Grocery and Market, a tailor and a tea room. In 1905 a fire in the market was extinguished by the newly formed permanent fire department, which had just moved into the new Municipal Building at Lake Street and Euclid.

The Chicago and North Western Railroad played an integral role in Oak Park's growth as a commuter suburb. The Chicago and Galena Union Railroad first connected the city to Oak Ridge in 1848, and as the village expanded during the seventies following the Chicago Fire, service continually improved to meet the demand.

As early as 1878 there were three morning trains (the 6:15 a.m. was called the "worky," the 7:15 and the "clerky," and the 8:15 a.m. the "shirky," with three trains at the end of the day for their homeward journey. By 1885 the North Western boasted 15 trains per day each way from 6:00 a.m. to 10:00 p.m.

In the 1890s this fine brick and stone station was built on Marion Street to replace the original makeshift depot (which had been nothing more than a baggage car with the wheels removed) that had been moved to the Marion Street site from River Forest

In 1872 Marion Street was the business center of the village and the first North Western depot was located there. In the early eighties, however, this brick depot was built at the Oak Park Avenue station by private subscription of property owners like James Scoville, who had their homes and businesses closer to this stop. The carriage and baggage entrance was on the North Blvd. side.

in 1871. Two pairs of flimsy gates were the only protection afforded pedestrians and every year there were numerous fatalities, until both the North Western Railroad and later the Lake Street Electric were elevated.

The Oak Park station of the Chicago Harlem and Batavia Railroad, better known as the "dummy" line. This railroad, which began operating in 1882 and lasted less than 25 years, had only six miles of tracks and ran on Randolph Street from 40th Street in Chicago to Harlem Avenue.

The railroad was intended to provide transportation to the cemeteries in Forest Park. The fare was 10 cents a trip to Oak Park and an extra 5 cents for a transfer to the street cars for the ride to Des Plaines Avenue.

The line was very undependable. At certain times of the year the trains would stop when water covered the tracks and extinguished the fire in the fire box. In the winter of 1885 the line was immobile for six weeks when the company failed to clear the tracks of snow.

The "dummy" line passed through many hands until 1901 when the Lake Street Elevated let the franchise expire and abandoned the line. The tracks along Randolph Street were removed in 1904. Today all that remains of the old "dummy" line are small plots of parkway where the stations stood on Randolph at Wisconsin, Oak Park, East, and Lombard Avenues.

Ridgeland School, built in 1879 on the east side of Cuyler between Ontario and Erie. In addition to the school, the self-contained community of Ridgeland boasted a brick community hall on Lake Street near Ridgeland that became the center of all the town's social life.

Residents of Ridgeland enjoyed such an active social life that people in Oak Park, Austin and River Forest flocked to the dances that were held regularly in the community hall. Special street cars were pressed into service on these nights to accommodate the revelers.

The Reporter often noted, "On Friday evening the Ridgeland Club will hold another of their fortnightly parties at the hall. The Cicero and Proviso Street Railway will as usual run cars to accommodate the guests."

Lake and Ridgeland business district looking northeast. In 1902, before Ridgeland and Oak Park had voted themselves out of Cicero Township and combined to form a single municipal government, the community of Ridgeland was a "silk-stocking" prosperous town.

This large tract north of the North Western tracks and east of East Avenue had been bought for approximately $700 per acre by James Scoville, W.B. Ogden, Joel Harvey, and Josiah Lombard, for whom some of the streets are named. It was later purchased by E.E. Cummings and subdivided in 1872.

Camille and Edward Merz shown in front of their home at 421 S. Lombard around 1900. As owners of a substantial house and automobile, the Merzes were undoubtedly active in one or more of the social clubs that met in the Ridgeland hall. There was a cycling club, a literary club, a cricket club, a tennis club and even a Republican club.

But elegant entertaining in Ridgeland was not restricted to clubs. A typical social item in the Reporter noted that "Mr. and Mrs. Hiram Coombs entertained almost all Ridgeland on Wednesday evening at the formal opening of their new home on Cuyler Avenue. During the evening supper was served by a Chicago caterer."

OAK PARK HIGH SCHOOL

Oak Park's first high school, a three story building designed for 350 students, on the southwest corner of Lake and East Avenue, was built by the elementary school district in 1891 to relieve overcrowding at the elementary school at Lake Street and Forest.

Until 1873 students were offered instruction only as far as the 8th grade. In that year the first high school curriculum was made available, and in 1877 the first graduating class had three members. The enrollment continued to grow and in 1891 this separate building, also called Central School (like its elementary counterpart), was built.

Graduating Class of 1909 in front of the arched Ontario Street entrance.

Oak Park-River Forest High School, with the main entrance on Ontario. That street was closed during the 1968 renovation and the main entrance was moved to Scoville Avenue.

The center portion of this building containing the arched entrance (see left) was built in 1907 to relieve overcrowding in the original high school building. The building was originally intended to be much larger, but because of delays that resulted in increased costs, only this first section was built in 1907. The additional wings shown in this photo were built sporadically until the mid-twenties.

During the 1890s, when discussion turned to the need for a larger building, it was agreed that operating two separate school programs within a single district was both unwieldy and unproductive. In 1899 the voters approved the establishment of a separate high school district composed of the two school districts known as Oak Park (Cicero) and River Forest (Proviso), to be directed by an elected board with levying power.

In 1905 this board proposed Ontario Street between East Avenue and Scoville as the site of the new high school. Architects for the original building were Patton & Spencer, who designed a building influenced by the Italian Renaissance and, although at least four other architectural firms worked on later additions, they all adhered to the original design.

High school biology lab in the early 1900s. A memo in an early science curriculum noted that it was "improper to discuss some aspects of science, especially biology, in a mixed group."

The Oak Park-River Forest High School stadium, which was built in 1924 in just 42 working days and without the use of any tax money. This 6000 seat stadium, still standing, is a visible tribute to the village's support of the high school.

The cost of the stadium was $112,500, which was raised by the sale of a unique type of bond backed only by receipts from athletic events. Later, when the bonds were paid, many of the holders donated the money they had invested back into the newly established scholarship fund and today seniors who receive scholarships from this fund are reaping the benefits of their generousity.

Room 338 in the old southwest wing was originally called the English Club Room and used for clubs, meetings and other gatherings. Today it is called the Hemingway Room in honor of the school's most famous graduate.

The fireplace has two terra-cotta shields on which are carved a quotation of Chaucer ("Gladly wolde he lerne, and gladly teche.") and the school crest containing the school motto, "Those things that are best." OPRF has maintained its tradition of academic excellence. During the 1986-87 school year. OPRF students achieved significantly higher scores on both ACT and SAT tests than the national average.

In this same year 13 students were selected as National Merit Finalists, another 40 were ranked as National Merit Commended, and 149 students were chosen as Illinois State Scholars.

Study hall in the 1920s. During this era boys were expected to wear jackets and could be sent from class for not wearing a tie.

An 1983 all-school assembly in the field house which was built in 1927. Prior to that time field houses had been built in just a few colleges and universities, and were almost unknown in secondary schools.

Through the years the field house has been the scene of spirited regional and conference competition in a variety of sports, including girls' and boys' basketball, volleyball, gymnastics, and indoor track.

A portion of the school's media center, which spans the second and third floor of the north wing. It as created in 1968 when that portion of the school was renovated, and today houses over 51,000 volumes, 300 periodicals, and thousands of films, slides, tapes, cassettes, and compact discs.

This media center is an invaluable learning tool for all students, whatever their course of study. The school requires a broad-based education of all its students, including courses in the practical arts and the fine and performing arts. In addition, special education programs and industrial and business education programs are also offered.

Over 86 percent of the graduates of the Class of 1987 enrolled in more than 174 different colleges, universities, community colleges and trade or technical schools.

Students at OPRF represent a rich variety of racial and ethnic backgrounds. Of the 3,047 students currently enrolled, 72.6 percent are white and 27.4 percent represent minorities.

A panoramic view of both the old and new high school building, looking northeast from the stadium during a memorial Day Assembly. In 1968 the new addition designed to increase student enrollment by 50 percent was built. Ontario Street was closed, the arched entrance of the main building was eliminated, and the main entrance was relocated on Scoville Avenue. A major renovation of the older portion of the school followed completion of this new facility.

For the past ten years commencement has been held in the stadium, weather permitting. Although seniors vote each year on the attire to be worn at graduation, it is an ongoing tradition that girls wear long white dresses and carry a dozen red roses, and boys wear dark suits and rose boutonnieres.

The athletic field is used for a variety of outdoor sports including football, baseball, and outdoor track. In 1981 the boys' baseball team was state champions an during the 1984, 1985 and 1986 seasons the team was state semifinalist. Coach Charles Kaiser was recently inducted into the American Baseball Coaches Association's Hall of Fame, an honor awarded to only 124 other amateur baseball coaches.

1922 senior girls' basketball team. The first recorded inter-scholastic girls' basketball game in Illinois was between Austin High School and Oak Park in 1886.

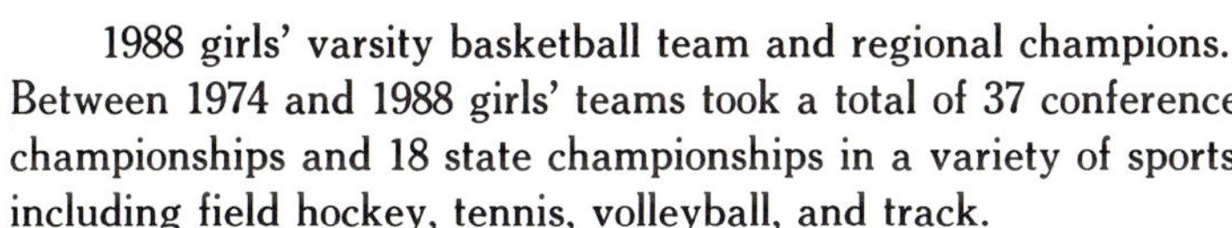

1988 girls' varsity basketball team and regional champions. Between 1974 and 1988 girls' teams took a total of 37 conference championships and 18 state championships in a variety of sports including field hockey, tennis, volleyball, and track.

1988 boys' varsity basketball team, second in conference for the season. Between 1974 and 1987 boys' teams captured a total of 66 conference championships in sports.

1988 OPRF varsity football team, participants in the state playoffs. Between 1974 and 1988 boys' varsity teams at OPRF took a total of 30 state championships.

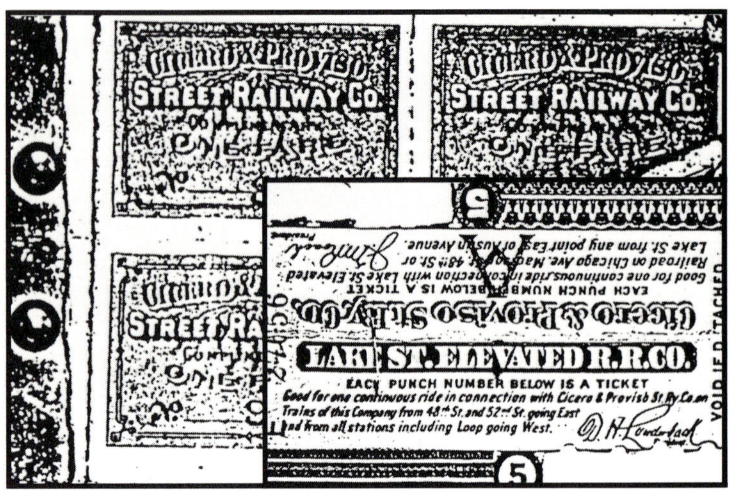

The "summer" trolley of the Cicero and Proviso Street Railway eastbound on Roosevelt Road. This open car had canvas curtains on the side which passengers could roll up to catch a breeze in the warm weather and close when it rained.

Commuters purchased monthly passes on the Cicero and Proviso Street Railway Company in much the same way as villagers riding the North Western do today. Complimentary passes were also given out to attract new riders.

The Cicero and Proviso Street Railway, a suburban system of electric street cars, was incorporated in 1889 and the first line was operated in 1891. This line had its terminal at Pulaski and Madison and ran west on Madison to Harlem, north to Lake Street, east on Lake to Cicero, south to Madison and back to Pulaski.

The company expanded rapidly and by 1895 there were electric street car lines on Chicago Avenue, Lake Street and Roosevelt Road going as far west as Des Plaines Avenue. And, although houses were still extremely sparse in this "south prairie," the speed of these electric street cars made it possible for more people to settle in this area and work downtown.

This Madison Street trolley stopping to pick up a passenger is eastbound at Ridgeland.

The Lake Street Elevated Company was incorporated in 1888, but it was not until 1901 that the Company was able to negotiate a franchise with the Cicero Township Board that extended the line west on South Blvd. all the way to Harlem Avenue. The road was built as an elevated to Laramie and then proceeded by an incline to the surface on South Blvd. west of Austin.

Until 1907 both the Lake Street "L" and North Western ran parallel at ground level in Oak Park. Unguarded grade crossings such as this one at Clinton Avenue were extremely dangerous and resulted in several deaths each year. By 1911 the North Western had elevated its tracks, but it was not until the 1950s that the Lake Street Elevated was actually "elevated" in Oak Park.

In 1899 the Chicago Consolidated Traction Company purchased several transportation companies including the Cicero and Proviso Street Railway Company. The Chicago Consolidated Tractions Company operated until 1913 when the name was changed to the Chicago and West Town Company. By the early thirties the street cars had been replaced by buses. The garage at Harvey and Lake Street that was recently demolished (to make way for a Dominick's food store) was built in 1924 to maintain the fleet of buses and cars serving the western suburbs.

These conductors and motormen are about to board their street car at Austin and Lake Street. Note the cowcatcher which was still a necessary piece of equipment in the unfenced prairies served by the street cars around the turn of the century.

Blase's Grocery, a fixture on Lake Street today as it has been since 1891. This is Blase's second store at 326-8 Lake (but showing the old numbering of 1003). The second from the right was Arthur Blase, son of the owner. All of the grocers doubled as volunteer firemen and when the alarm sounded at the Ridgeland firehouse at Lake and Lombard they doffed their aprons and made a dash for the station.

Lake Street looking east at Marion on what must have been a warm summer day in the 1890s. The woman heading toward Schneider's Grocery on the east side of Marion and Lake is protecting herself from the sun with a parasol, while the shopkeepers have lowered their awnings to keep out the sun. The Steiner building is one the west side of Marion and the soaring spire of the First Congregational Church is visible two blocks away. Police and fire protection was just around the corner in a frame building shared by both departments.

CHAPTER III

FROM
WEALTH
TO
WOE

1903-1929

In 1902 officials of the newly independent village of Oak Park were anxious to put past skirmishes with Cicero Township behind them and lead the community into a new era of growth and prosperity.

One of the village board's first acts of municipal muscle-flexing was to build the village hall at Lake Street and Euclid Avenue over the objections of west side residents, who thought the hall should be located further west on Marion Street where the population was centered at that time. Anticipating expansion to the south, east and north, the board held firm to its decision and the new municipal building opened in 1904.

The board's vision of a community that would expand dramatically in the first two decades of the twentieth century, both geographically and population-wise, proved accurate. The population doubled every ten years, from just under 10,000 in 1900 to nearly 40,000 by 1920.

The ethnic composition of this growing population remained just as homogeneous as it had been in the past. In 1910 the foreign born made up only 21 percent of the total population of 19,444, and 88 percent of these foreign born residents came from England, Scotland, Ireland, Canada, Germany and Scandinavia. Few Oak Parkers were part of the new emigration from eastern Europe and only 166 blacks lived in the village.

Some of the growth occurred on the north side when areas as far north as Division Street were built up, but the most dramatic growth occurred south of Madison Street. This was due in large part to builders such as Thomas Hulburt and Seward Gunderson, who bought large sections of the "south prairie," then divided and subdivided it into tracts on which they built affordable housing for the working man and his family.

By 1915 abut one third of the population lived south of Madison Street, a remarkable growth in an area that ten years earlier had been a prairie.

Real estate activity and the building of single family homes was at a new high between 1906 and 1917. Between 300 and 400 building permits for new homes were issued annually until the pre-war peak was reached in 1915. Construction then declined rapidly until 1918 when only 44 new home permits were issued.

Construction of large multi-unit apartments boomed during the twenties despite the opposition of many village residents and realtors. Oak Park's first zoning ordinance, passed in 1921, controlled but did not prevent the construction of these large buildings and much of Oak Park's present apartment stock dates from that decade.

Seward Gunderson was the master in promoting the advantages of home ownership and his newspaper advertisement bore headlines such as: "People who ever lived in their own homes never go back to renting if they can help it."

Gunderson's new home promotions, which were always directed at the male breadwinner, didn't mince words: "Your interest in civic affairs is suddenly and vastly increased and rendered definite instead of theoretical. You instantly become a better citizen. In a way, the renter - the lifelong tenant - is a piece of driftwood, subject to the many buffeting gales, while the home owner is a staunch ship, upon the same sea of life."

To counter this, proselytizing landlords promised tenants apartments that "have been built with the idea that the dweller in an apartment is entitled to some conveniences and to as good light and as good air as the man who lives in a house." Home-like features such as porches, windows that looked out on open areas, modern plumbing, gas and electric fixtures were all highlighted.

But despite this building boom everyone was not well-housed or well-fed. In the twenties often as many as 50 unemployed laborers were housed in the jail during the cold winter months.

In April, 1917 when the United States entered World War I, all village activities became centered on the war effort. A local draft board was set up and all unmarried males between the ages of 20 and 30 were quick to respond. In 1918 the official tabulation showed 1,950 enlisted men in the service from Oak Park.

A huge patriotic rally at the high school kicked off Oak Park's war efforts in 1917. Survivors of the Civil War were honored, bands marched and played, and the speeches lasted until after 11:00 p.m. Villagers enthusiastically subscribed to Victory Liberty Loans and followed the guidelines laid down by the U.S. Food Administration for wheatless, meatless, sugar-saving and fat-saving day, in order to conserve food which was used to feed the Allies as well as our own soldiers. A Red Cross chapter headquartered in the YMCA directed the war efforts of numerous women's church and social groups.

When the war was finally over, in 1919, a gigantic celebration was held to welcome returning soldiers and sailors from the war. An estimated 40,000 people lined the parade route and took part in the parade. A house-to-house canvas by old veterans was made to ensure that every returning veteran had an invitation.

The parade ended in the high school field where three bands gave a concert. Following the festivities the veterans were given a chicken dinner and in the evening the "lid was off" with professional entertainment in the high school auditorium.

On Armistice Day, 1925 the War Memorial to the Oak Park men who served in World War I was dedicated in Scoville Park. Funds for this monument were raised by private subscription. A special tablet bears the names of the 56 who gave their lives.

The opening decades of the twentieth century were generally a time of prosperity and growth in the village; but beneath the surface of the idyllic picture painted by Oak Park's most ardent supporters there were conflicts and strains involving social, economic and political issues, that threatened to divide the community.

There were many villagers, primarily in the south end, who were dissatisfied with village services and favored annexation of Oak Park to Chicago. In 1910 and 1911 the question of annexation appeared on the ballot and both times it was defeated.

This sectional antagonism continued for several more years as south siders organized the New Citizen Party and slated candidates for the 1916 village board election. Running on the platform that the New Citizen Party "stands for the cause

of the many and not of the few," candidates made accusations that Oak Park was being run by a "coterie of millionaires" from the north and central parts of the community.

Although the New Citizen Party got 30 percent of the vote, the movement seemed to stall after that election, probably because village services were beginning to catch up with the tremendous growth that had occurred in south Oak Park.

Other changes that had an impact in Oak Park after 1902 and made many residents apprehensive included new entertainments such as jazz, movies and speakeasies, which were increasingly available in Chicago and other suburbs.

The question of Sunday movies appeared on the ballot in 1917, 1923 and 1925, and was defeated each time. In newspaper interviews opponents successfully argued that they were "tempting, thrilling, lust-appealing adventures which will attract our young people and tempt them to attend this form of entertainment rather than the soul-stirring, mental stimulation derived from attending church services or other organizations created for spiritual uplift."

By 1932 opponents were fighting a losing battle and the referendum to allow Sunday movies passed with most residents failing to see the alleged evil in them.

The increased popularity of the auto and the spread of new transit systems, especially in the south end of the village, also served as catalysts for continued growth and change. In 1901 the Lake Street Elevated was opened to Harlem Avenue and in 1905 the Metropolitan West Side Elevated was extended through Harrison Street to serve the south end of the village.

Oak Parkers had already begun to eagerly accept the auto before the war, but in the 1920s auto ownership became even more widespread and the development of more and better roads made villagers less dependent on mass transit.

Shopping patterns also began to change as department stores and large retail chains began to locate on Lake Street. Now the stores came to the customers, rather than the customers always traveling downtown to the stores. The Hub was the first large Chicago store to open an Oak Park branch in 1927, followed by Marshall Field & Company and The Fair in 1929.

In October, 1929 local businesses were booming and most villagers were in a mood to buy. When Marshall Field & Company opened their new branch at Lake Street and Harlem Avenue a throng of 40,000 shoppers from Chicago and surrounding suburbs jammed the store during the opening week.

Also in October, hundreds of Oak Park ladies attended a fur fashion show and tea at Madame Pankow's, a leading village furrier, to view the new fall styles in fur. Snow Brothers, 1011 South Blvd. advertised that with a new Ford you had the "comfortable assurance that everything is just right."

But, of course, after October 29, 1929, life would not be "just right" for most villagers as the effect of the Depression began to ripple through the community. It's unlikely that many of the women who attended Madame Pankow's show followed through with the purchase of a coat. Most were grateful if their savings were left intact or some member of their family just had a job.

By 1902 residents of both Oak Park and Ridgeland had voted themselves out of Cicero Township and formed a separate village complete with president and trustees.

The new board met both in Scoville Institute and at 122 N. Oak Park Avenue while plans were drawn up for a new village hall. After a great deal of controversy, the site at Euclid Avenue and Lake Street was selected and Prairie School architect E. E. Roberts was chosen to design it.

A protest meeting of a hundred angry west side residents was held in the Warrington Opera House on Marion Street. They claimed that since 60 percent of the population and businesses were located between Oak Park Avenue and Harlem Avenue, the municipal building should be located further west; but with an eye toward expansion to the south, east and north, the board held firm to its decision. The new municipal building was completed in 1904.

Village fathers and telephone company officials marking the opening of the Chicago Telephone Company's new office on Lake Street near Euclid Avenue, across the street from the municipal building.

The first village telephone was installed in 1895 above the Oak Park Bank on Marion Street and North Blvd. The office was later transferred to Lovett's Drug Store on the corner of Lake and Marion Streets, with one operator in charge.

By 1901 there were nearly 1,000 telephones in Oak Park and the following year the company moved into its own building at 118 Marion. But these facilities were soon outgrown and by 1915 this larger building became district headquarters for the Chicago Telephone Company. Another milestone occurred about 1924 when village prefixes were shortened from "Oak Park" into "Euclid" and "Village."

Photo courtesy of Village of Oak Park

Around the turn of the century many wealthy villagers kept Shetland ponies for the amusement of their children. This 1909 photo taken in front of the home of W. R. Harvey, 616 Forest Avenue (now 426), shows Elizabeth Harvey and Jasper Redmond in their elaborately decorated cart, which was a prize winner at John Farson's Oak Park Horse Show.

By 1918 the auto had replaced the horse and carriage for both adults and children. In this photo little Virginia Roos is using the driveway of her Oak Park home to practice "driving" her own automobile.

Oak Park Avenue looking north from North Blvd. around 1915. By this time electric arc lighting had replaced the gas lamps in the business districts, and the busy thoroughfare (an ungraded road just a few years earlier) had been paved with cedar blocks. This surface proved too bumpy for villagers out for a ride in their new autos, and by 1910 the cedar blocks had disappeared.

Oak Park was beginning to rival Marion Street as the business center of the village. In 1902 the Scoville Building (seen in the background on the east side of Oak Park Avenue), a three-story building consisting of stores, offices and apartments, was completed.

The newly formed Avenue State Bank occupied the site of
what is now Springer's in this building until 1921, when the Bank
erected its own building half a block south on the site of the old
Chicago Suburban Water & Light Company plant. The power
plant and reservoir had been razed some time after 1912 when
Oak Park began receiving water from Chicago.

In 1908 Charles B. Scoville built the Masonic Bank (seen in
the background on the west side of Oak Park Avenue). Second
floor offices were leased to Masonic lodges and businesses while
first floor stores were rented to retail firms.

Clerks in frock coats in Nissen and Puckner's Grocery, who
respectfully catered to the culinary needs of the carriage trade.
The store was located on the first floor of the Masonic Block.

Butchers at Nissen and Puckner's Grocery cut meat to order
under the watchful eyes of customers.

In 1921 the Oak Park Board of Trustees passed the village's first zoning ordinance in an attempt to thwart entrepreneurs who were thoughtlessly destroying many landmark pioneer homes, in their haste to erect "up-to-date" buildings.

Homeowners' anger over a proposed 52-unit apartment on the corner of Euclid and Pleasant, an area of substantial single family homes, was the catalyst that resulted in the drafting of a zoning ordinance.

In an attempt to maintain property values and promote orderly development, trustees designated which sections were to be developed exclusively for single family and multi-family residential, commercial and light industrial use, and also made an extensive list of businesses and activities that were not permitted in each area.

Retail businesses were banned in single family residential areas but neighborhood grocery stores in place prior to the ordinance, such as this one on the 700 block of Highland, were allowed to remain.

In 1915 the village board had passed another landmark ordinance mandating that residences in the village be numbered according to a new system. The new law placed "north" and "south" before names of north and south streets and indicated that the Chicago & North Western tracks would be the dividing line, except on Austin Blvd. where the dividing line would be Madison Street to coincide with Chicago's numbering system.

Looking north from Ontario at the multi-unit apartments lining Oak Park Avenue, which were built in the 1920s, a halcyon time for builders when concrete was king and the cement trucks never stopped rolling. Out of 350 municipalities around the country, Oak Park was second only to Chicago in new construction, pouring foundations for everything from one-car garages to 45-unit apartment buildings.

Over 200 plasterers, carpenters and plumbers worked on the block-long Santa Maria apartments (right) which were completed in May, 1924. In addition to this new construction, Oak Park was also transformed by major street and alley paving, sewer building and a complete new street lighting system.

This rush to build multi-family housing wasn't universally applauded. Flats, as a menace to home life, was the topic at a meeting of the Nineteenth Century Woman's Club.

"How can a family maintain the old sweet intimacy when it is forced to share its home with from six to 20 other families under the same roof?" asked Ida Stearns. "There is nothing more pitiable than a family of children which ought to have to benefit of open air and a big yard, forced to spend their childhood in a four or five room flat," she concluded.

Once the sign went up advertising that this site at 1024-30 Randolph could be developed for apartments, it was only a matter of time before these early Oak Park buildings came down. The thoughtless destruction of many of these pioneer homes was of no concern to the entrepreneurs who financed large apartments.

"Some of the old buildings now being wrecked have outlived their usefulness and are now making way for more up-to-date buildings," said a local realtor in a newspaper interview.

"This is but another sign of the westward expansion of Chicago which is changing Oak Park from a small village of homes to a large city with up-to-date commercial centers and superb residential districts," he continued. "There still remains a number of antiquated frame buildings on Lake Street that are going to be torn down. They are a definite handicap to the retail business of this section."

In 1889 Frank Lloyd Wright, a 22-year-old architectural firebrand who worked for the firm of Adler and Sullivan, purchased a lot to build a home for his bride Catherine on the northern edge of the village - and Oak Park has never been the same.

It was in this home, and later in the attached studio built in 1898, that Wright, considered an architectural maverick whose work revolutionized residential design around the world, developed his Prairie Style of architecture. The freeflowing spaces of this style, the interweaving of interior and exterior, broad overhanging eaves, groundhugging horizontals marked by long bands of windows, and the use of natural materials and earthtoned colors all changed the nature of the American home.

Today more than 50,000 visitors come to Oak Park annually to view the rich legacy of buildings designed by the genius who died in 1959 at the age of 92. The restored Frank Lloyd Wright Home and Studio is a National Historic Landmark and the surrounding area, which contains 25 Wright-designed structures, has been designated a National Historic District.

The village contains more buildings of national and international significance per capita than any other community in the United States and is a living museum of 19th and 20th century American architecture.

Wright used both his home and studio as a laboratory to experiment with space, form, light, materials, furnishings and decorative arts. The building was constantly in transition, showcasing the architect's evolving philosophy of design.

Although Wright left Oak Park in 1909, he returned in 1911 to remodel his home and studio into rental space which provided his family with an income. He sold the property in 1925 and ownership passed through a number of hands until the home and studio was finally subdivided into as many as seven apartments.

In 1974 the property was offered for sale again and rumors began to circulate that it was to be razed, dismantled and moved, or suffer some other indignity. Most Oak Parkers have a well-developed sense of the importance of Wright's legacy to the village, and so a group of interested citizens hastily formed the Frank Lloyd Wright Home and Studio Foundation.

The Foundation persuaded the National Trust for Historic Preservation to purchase the property. Today the National Trust works in partnership with the Foundation, which has sole responsibility for the operation and restoration of the Home and Studio with private and federal funds.

In 1986 the $2.1 million, 12-year restoration of this National Historic Landmark was finally completed. The building has been restored to its 1909 design, the last year Wright lived and worked on the property.

The project was an enormous undertaking, comprising some 15 planning, design and construction phases. Over the past 12 years the project involved some 30 architects and other design professionals, 80 contractors, craftsmen and major suppliers, more than 350 individuals from the building industry, the support of a hundred board members, 50 staff members, and in excess of 1,000 volunteers. Financial contributions in the form of grants and gifts came from members, visitors, corporations, foundations and the federal government.

In 1889 Wright built this home for his bride Catherine on the prairie at what was then the northern end of the village. The home was set back from the street creating a sense of privacy.

By 1898 Wright had built his studio, which was attached to his home by a covered passageway, so that work and family life could intermingle. The draftsmen ate lunch with the family and the children grew up in an architect's office.

But by 1909 this unity of family and professional life had become a burden. Wright separated from his wife, closed the studio and left Oak Park with the wife of a client to seek a new independence. He did return in 1911,however, to remodel the studio into rental space for boarders who provided his family with an income.

As his family grew, Wright began a series of major remodelings. Above the kitchen wing he built this fabulous playroom for his six children. This massive room with a barrel-vaulted ceiling has recessed balconies and a fireplace mural by Giannini depicting a tale from the Arabian Nights. The skylight is covered with decorative wooden grilles.

The master bedroom of Wright's 1889 home, restored to its 1909 design. The semi-circular wall mural that had been painted over numerous times was restored, the art glass windows recreated, and Wright-designed lighting fixtures were reproduced.

All photos courtesy of Frank Lloyd Wright Home and Studio Foundation.

Frank Lloyd Wright's drafting room, perhaps the most dramatic addition to the complex, was added in 1898. The room is two stories high with clerestory windows and an octagonal balcony hung on a chain harness that looks down from all eight sides.

Artisans such as Wright's stained-glass designers worked on the balcony, while the draftsmen labored on the ground floor room which is centered around a massive fireplace that "has the air of a charming living room" according to one visitor. Here Wright orchestrated a steady stream of commissions from clients "willing to try the uncharted."

The intimate space of the inglenook near the entry contrasts with more open spaces in Wright's home. The arched fireplace symbolizes the "heart" of the home and of his family.

The restored 1895 dining room, where lighting and furniture are an integral part of the design, is rich in decorative details. The furnishings are all Wright-designed originals, including his son Llewellyn's high chair.

Unity Temple, designed by Wright in 1905, has been designated a National Historic Landmark. The monumental concrete exterior of this building contrasts with the open, light-filled interior. Wright was a member of this Unitarian congregation, and after the first church was destroyed by fire he was asked to design a new building on a budget of only $45,000.

Wright solved the problem by coming up with an entirely innovative design that included the strength and dignity appropriate to a church but eliminated the expense (and potential for fire) of a soaring roof and spire.

The architect preferred to have the building referred to as a "temple" rather than a church because the simplicity of his design suggested an ancient temple; but it is the way he let the space inside shape the building that makes Unity Temple so unique.

The Nathan Moore Home, a huge twin-gabled Tudor home overlaid with geometric and oriental shapes, was designed by Wright in 1895 and is certainly one of his most eccentric-looking buildings. The house was almost destroyed by fire in 1922 and Moore asked Wright to redesign his house. At that time the architect, who had been away from Oak Park for more than ten years, had just completed the Imperial Hotel in Tokyo and utilized some of the same oriental motifs that he had used in the hotel.

This birdseye view west from Oak Park Avenue and Madison Street was taken in 1903. Madison Street did not begin to develop as a business district until around 1910 when large tracts of the "south prairie" were subdivided for housing by builders such as Thomas H. Hurlburt, who built about 200 homes on large lots in 1906, and Seward Gunderson, who built more than 600 homes between 1906 and 1920.

By 1915 about one third of the village population lived south of Madison Street, a remarkable growth for an area that ten years earlier had been a prairie.

John E. James in front of his stucco works and real estate office at 914 Gunderson. This small building was bulldozed in1956 to make way for the Congress Expressway. James is the founder of what is today W.R. James Realtors, one of the oldest family-owned businesses in the village.

In 1896 he began a small contracting business that supplied stucco and concrete to Frank Lloyd Wright and Seward Gunderson for their respective and totally different homes. To keep his crews busy during the winter James began purchasing lots and building homes himself.

In 1919 his son Walter James took over this real estate portion of the business. In 1975 Walter James was designated Realtor Emeritus by the National Association of Realtors for more than 50 years of service in the profession. Today his son Bob James heads the family firm.

Photo courtesy of W.R. James Realtors.

In 1907 Adolph Steigerwald came from Chicago with his wife
Caroline and their four children, Kathryn, Frank, Alfred and
Gladys to build his home and business, a general store at 108
Madison. The gentleman wearing a hat is a customer.

The Will Cotton Laundry at Kenilworth and Madison opened
around 1912 to meet the needs of a village population that was
expanding rapidly to the south.

These Are a Few of Our Oak Park Homes

Gunderson Station, Met. "L" (5c fare), on Elmwood, 64th
and Gunderson Aves., between Madison and Harrison Sts.

Have Others — Six to ten rooms — *ready now* — or will
build to suit you — ready *next Spring*

Prices Right   Cash or Terms

S. T. GUNDERSON & SONS, *Home Builders*

810 Chamber of Commerce   Branch Office on Premises

Throughout Gunderson's two tracts he planted 1,200 Carolina poplars 25 feet apart. In addition to the stucco exteriors shown in this picture prospective homeowners were given the added choices of shingle or wood. Gunderson had extensive lumber holdings that helped keep building costs down.

The builder intended his tracts to be family-oriented and had no use for apartments. The homeowner's deed of sale included a clause prohibiting the future building of apartments.

During this same era when Frank Lloyd Wright was achieving national prominence with his innovative homes that generally only the wealthy could purchase, another Oak Park builder was constructing large tracts of comfortable family homes which the average working man could afford.

Between 1906 and 1920 Seward Gunderson built more than 600 homes in the village for prices ranging from $4,000 to $12,000. Most of these homes were built in two large tracts of land bounded by Roosevelt Road, Madison Street, Harlem Avenue and Ridgeland Avenue.

Although Gunderson built many homes at one time, there is none of the cookies cutter sameness found in so many modern subdivisions. He offered 42 distinctive models with 15 separate floor plans and all homes, regardless of size and cost, included five stained glass windows, oak floors, six closets, bay windows and a solid oak built-in sideboard in the dining room.

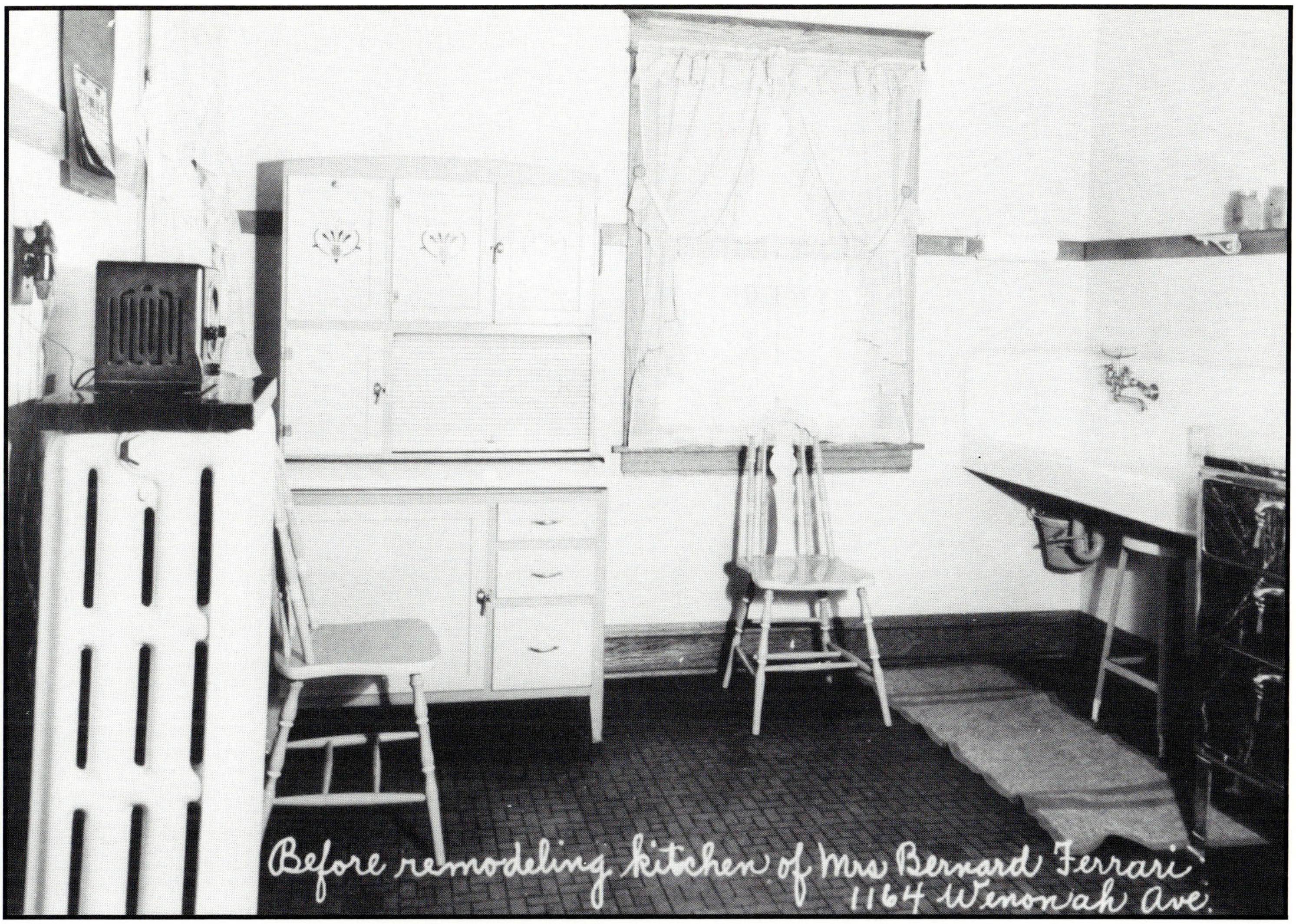

The caption of the first photograph reads:

A well equipped 1920's kitchen in a home at 1164 Wenonah.
The study of the domestic sciences for girls was raised to an art during this period. Women who attended a 1924 meeting of the North Oak Park Women's Club listened as a lady from Peoples Gas Light and Coke Company exhorted them on the proper use of their time. With mathematical precision they were advised to devote 50 percent of their day to food preparation, 15 percent to laundry, 15 percent to cleaning, leaving 20 percent for chores that didn't fall into any of these catagories.

Seward Gunderson is credited with pioneering modern construction techniques such as steel beam supports, concrete block foundations and large front porches on stone piers shown in this photo.

Gunderson was famed for the quality of his work. Once when he found a contractor had mislaid a steel post by three inches, he gave the man two hours to jack the house up and place it properly. He is also credited with the raising of the kitchen sink to today's height after watching a maid bending over a low sink that was the standard at the time. He realized what a strain it put on her back and raised the sinks in his homes accordingly.

For many years Gunderson lived in one of his own homes in the center of one of his tracts. When he retired the homeowners gave him a banquet to show their appreciation for the quality of his work.

Out of desperation Burroughs began to write. "I began to write not for any particular love of writing. It was because I had a wife and two babies- a combination which does not work well without money", he said later.

Burroughs sold his first story, "Under the Moon of Mars", to All Story magazine for $400 in 1912. Buoyed by that success he spent his spare time reading Jack London, Kipling, and Stanley's, "In Darkest Africa". He had little confidence in a story he wrote evenings on the back of envelopes and was amazed when he received $700 for it. It was called "Tarzan of the Apes" and appeared in the October, 1912 issue of All Story.

Between 1912 and 1919 Edgar Rice Burroughs, the creator of Tarzan, wrote 22 Tarzan books in Oak Park. Burroughs had moved to his father's "country home" at 414 Augusta in 1910 at the lowest point of his life. He was 29, married for four years and had drifted from job to job unable to support himself, let alone a family. When his second child was born he had to pawn his watch to buy food.

The lean days for Burrough were over. He moved his family into a stately home at 700 N. Linden where he continued to write his increasingly popular books.

In 1918 Burroughs was appointed a major in the Illinois Reserve Militia. The militia saw no active service during World War I and was organized primarily for local protection against any pro-German elements.

Following the war Burroughs moved his family to 47,000 acre ranch outside Los Angeles. He formed a company, Burroughs, Inc., which marketed Tarzan books, toys, comics, radio serials, films and fan clubs.

The Dole-Cheney mansion, 220 N. Euclid Avenue currently owned by the Park District of Oak Park and used for weddings, receptions, corporate meetings, and civic and cultural events, was a private residence for most of its 75 year history.

This elegant home was commissioned by C.A. Sharpe in 1913 and was designed by Charles E. White, a student of Frank Lloyd Wright. According to the Hasbrouck Sprague Survey of Historic Architecture in Oak Park, the house is of Simplified Rectilinear Style and, architecturally, "is of very high quality, highly original significance beyond the Chicago area, either nationally or internationally."

The estate was purchased from Sharpe by Andrew Dole in 1922 shortly after his marriage to Mary Hooker when both were in their fifties. Dole founded the Dole Valve Company in Chicago in 1906, and for 60 years was also associated with the Hooker Glass & Paint Company, serving as chairman of the board until his death in 1940.

Andrew and Mary Dole were active in the community and well -known for their numerous civic and charitable interests. The Doles are perhaps best known for their purchase of a former Congregational church at Augusta Blvd. and Cuyler which they donated to the village for use as the north branch of the Oak Park Library, now popularly called the Dole Branch.

When Mary Dole died in 1949 she left the 38-room mansion to her niece, Elizabeth Cheney, who had lived with the Doles since the death of her parents when she was 10. In 1975 she deeded the property to the Park District with the provision that it maintain the property during her lifetime. Following her death in 1985 the Park District has made the estate available to the community for a variety of civic, social and cultural events.

This two acre estate located in central Oak Park includes beautifully landscaped grounds, a greenhouse and a 6-room coachhouse, all surrounded by a decorative iron fence.

The living room of the Dole-Cheney mansion in the 1930s. Other rooms include a large foyer, dining room, library, solariium and oriental room. Many of Elizabeth Cheney's exquisite furnishings including oriental art objects, antiques, books and paints remain in the mansion and bring to life a gracious and bygone era.

The first photograph ever taken of the Borrowed Time Club. The name of the group of men who had passed the age of 70 was derived from a remark often made by Father Robbins, "I owe no man a dollar but am sadly in debt to Father Time." Robbins organized the group of men who met informally in his harness shop as early as the 1870's.

This photo was taken on September 9, 1904 in front of the home of Elijah Hoard, 125 N. Marion Street (now the northwest corner or Marion and Westgate). Seated in the front row is Elijah Hoard (with crutches) who served as honorary president; Father Robbins (holding hat), presidents; and Dr. Orin Peake, Oak Park's first physician and druggist.

Although only two autos are seen in this 1914 photo of Chicago Avenue looking west from Austin Boulevard, the automobile had already altered the lives of many villages.

Area merchants credited the auto with the growth of local business. Reporting that December, 1913 had seen the "best Christmas trade ever in Oak Park", one shop owner noted that the increasing number of autos enabled Oak Parkers to shop locally rather than take the train to the city. The auto was viewed as a stimulation to family life by encouraging family outings and activities. By 1917 there were 2,372 autos registered in Oak Park, about one for every 17 residents.

The Gale automobile in front of 538 N. Euclid in 1909. The auto, which was manufactured in Galesburg, Illinois from 1904 to 1906, scarcely caused Henry Ford any sleepless nights before the company went out of business.

By 1911 many villagers had become so incensed about "speeding" autos that it was seriously proposed that "bumps" be built into the pavement of every block to slow them down.

According to the proposal "these bumps should be worked out by an engineer so they will not jolt passengers or damage a car when it is going under 15 mph. Over that speed, however, the bumps should be constructed so that the passengers are bumped up to the canopy and the car is badly jolted."

In the late twenties motorists purchased new tires and had their autos serviced at this Sinclair station and tire store at 1115 Chicago Avenue. The tire store is now occupied by Giordano's resturant and the service station is the site of New Era Construction. *Photo courtesy of Village of Oak Park.*

Gas stations began appearing on vacant lots throughout the village to service the growing number of autos in the village. This Shell station at Madison and Harvey was built in the early twenties.

Photo courtesy of Village of Oak Park

The Oak Park Art League, a landmark for more than 50 years at 720 Chicago Avenue. The League was formed in 1921 in the home of Carl Krafft, the League's first president, and met at various locations including the Frank Lloyd Wright Home and Studio.

In 1937 the League found a permanent home in this building which was originally the coach house for the large Queen Anne home at 508 N. Oak Park Avenue. E.E. Roberts designed both the home and coach house and was also responsible for the 1937 renovation of the coach house.

Photo courtesy of Oak Park Art League.

Ernest Hemingway's mother, Grace Hall Hemingway, was a member of the Board of Directors when the Art League moved into its permanent home and is pictured here in front of the line leading the way into the new building,
Photo courtesy of Oak Park Art League

From the beginning the Art League has maintained an art school staffed by an impressive faculty of artists and offering classes for both adults and children. These young artists are hard at work in a class in the 1940's.
Photo courtesy of Oak Park Art League

Ernest Hemingway's birthplace, now 339 North Oak Park Avenue. Ruth Bagley Burchard, who lived behind the Hemingways, recalled Hemingway's father had promised that "if the baby is a boy I'll come out on the porch and blow my cornet".

Sure enough, on July 21, 1899 a triumphant trumpet call rang out from Oak Park Avenue and her mother called, "The Hemingways have a boy!" It was never clear what form the announcement would have taken had the baby been a girl.

Ernest Hemingway's boyhood home, 600 North Kenilworth. The Hemingways built this comfortable 8-bedroom house at the corner of Iowa and Kenilworth in 1906 for their growing family.

Hemingway, the second oldest of six children and the only boy until the birth of his younger brother Leicester, who was 15 years his junior, had a bedroom to himself on the third floor where he wrote some of his earliest stories for Tabula, the Oak Park High School year book.

Grace Hemingway, who had briefly pursued a career in grand opera before her marriage, added an acoustically perfect conservatory on the north side of this house which she used for music lessons and recitals.

The Hemingways spent every summer at Windemere, their summer home on Walloon Lake in northern Michigan. Dr. Clarence Hemingway, one of the founders of Oak Park Hospital and head of its obstetrics department, was also an avid outdoorsman, expert in hunting and fishing. During these Michigan summers he taught Ernest how to properly handle a gun, how to tie flies, how to dress fish and fowl, how to use an axe and the rudiments of physical courage.

But, however close father and son were during Hemingway's childhood, Clarence Hemingway, like his wife, was not comfortable with the direction his son's creativity was taking him.

A half-dozen copies of his second book, "In Our Time," written in Paris in 1924, were sent to and returned unopened by his father because the book dealt with venereal disease, a topic "no gentleman would discuss in public" according to his outraged father.

Hemingway's graduation picture in the 1917 Tabula. Hemingway wrote the Class Prophecy and Edward Wagenknecht, distinguished literary critic, writer and teacher was the Valedictorian. In his chapter on Hemingway in "Cavalcade of the American Novel" Wagenknecht enlarged upon the idea that Ernest was the average boy-next-door.

"Hemingway was a handsome, friendly and courteous boy who seemed equally enthusiastic about the sermons of the famous Dr. William Barton of the First Congregational Church and the performances of the Chester Wallace Players at the Warrington Theatre."

"I have since read that he was lonely in high school, that he had once run away from home and that he was sometimes regarded as a 'tough guy.' These things may or may not have been true; all I can say is that there was nothing in my contacts with Hemingway to cause me to suspect them. I had no classmate whom I recall with greater pleasure."

Shortly after graduation Hemingway went to Italy as an ambulance driver, where he was severely wounded by shrapnel. He returned to Oak Park to recuperate and appeared at a high school assembly to speak of his experiences.

Edith Cummings Conley, who was several years behind Hemingway, recalled that he cut a romantic figure for his impressionable audience. "Ernie was thin and very handsome," she said. "he came in limping with a cane and spoke so eloquently that five boys immediately left school to join the ambulance corps in Italy."

HEMINGWAY SPEAKS TO HIGH SCHOOL

With Italian Ambulance Service of Red Cross—Later Commissioned in Italian Army

WOUNDED IN PUSH ON PIAVE

By Edwin Wells

Lieut. Ernest M. Hemingway '17, late of the Italian Ambulance Service of the American Red Cross and then of the Italian Army spoke of his experiences in Italy at assembly last Friday. Caroline Bagley a classmate of the speaker introduced him to an audience the greater part of which already knew him.

"Stein" as he has been nicknamed, had lost none of the manner of speech which made his Ring Lardner letters for the Trapeze of several

Hemingway wearing a powdered wig in the uncharacteristic role of dandy in the class play, "Beau Brummel." His awareness of the arts was fostered by his mother, Grace, who saw that all her children had music lessons and encouraged them to attend concerts, operas and plays that came to Chicago.

But Grace Hemingway's appreciation of the arts and literature was tempered by her prudery and Victorian sense of what was "suitable." Edith Striker, Ernest's seventh grade teacher, recalled this mother coming to Holmes School one day to object to Jack London's "Call of the Wild." "It's not the kind of book young people should be reading," she said.

She was never able to understand her son's starkly realistic creativity and later, whenever anyone mentioned that they had read Hemingway's latest book or short story, Mrs. Hemingway's only comment was, "I never read any of Ernie's books."

The Oak Park-River Forest High School swim team; Hemingway is second from left in the front row. In addition to swimming the 1917 Tabula listed many other activities in which Hemingway participated including the track team, football, orchestra (he played the cello), Burke Debating Club, class play, Trapeze and Tabula. The caption under his picture in Tabula reads: "None is to be found more clever than Ernie."

Hemingway with Paul Haas on one of the many long hikes he frequently took with his high school classmates. The area around the Des Plaines River and the drainage canal that ran through Summit were just two of their destinations.

Hemingway's childhood in the years leading up to World War I was outwardly idyllic. His family fitted comfortably into the placid lifestyle of the village which, at that time, was considered as both "silk stocking" and "strait-laced" by outsiders. Ripples, much less waves, in these tranquil waters were definitely not encouraged.

Although as a boy Hemingway gave every appearance of conformity, it is interesting to speculate that it might have been this very image of propriety against which he would later rebel.

Hemingway never "returned" to his home town in the real sense of the word. But in 1952 he commented, "I had a wonderful novel to write about Oak Park and never would because I did not want to hurt living people."

Hemingway (right) with John Gehlmann and Sue Lowrey in the picture of the Trapeze staff in the 1917 issue of Tabula, the school yearbook. Hemingway was one of six Trapeze editors and also worked as a reporter.

Some of his earliest stories were published in the Tabula including "A Matter of Colour," a humorous boxing tale told by an old fight manager to a youthful listener, and another story that was a bloody tale of mayhem and suicide set in the north woods.

In 1902 a group of nine men met to organize a YMCA in Oak Park. Following the lead of his late father, whose generous gifts had made possible so many public buildings, Charles B. Scoville donated the lot at what is now 156 N. Oak Park Avenue as the site of the new "Y" and also make a substantial contribution to the building fund.

The new building was dedicated in 1904 and the following year the facilities, including what was then the second largest indoor pool in the country, were opened to women.

During World War II the YMCA was host to a chapter of the Red Cross and offered free privileges to visiting servicemen. Recreational activities for swing shift and night shift war workers were also available. In 1954 the present YMCA at Marion Street and Randolph was opened and the original building was sold to the Emmaus Bible School.

Ernest Hemingway attended the Saturday morning series of talks given by his father, Dr. Clarence Hemingway, at the Oak Park YMCA on a variety of subjects of interest to young boys. This admission ticket lists the topics, all dealing with the outdoors, covered by Dr. Hemingway in his weekly series.

BOYS' MEETINGS
at the
Oak Park Y. M. C. A.

Saturday mornings, 10:00 o'clock

In charge of the
KNIGHTS OF THE TRIANGLE.
All boys 12 - 16 years old are invited.

Initiation of those attending all meetings during any month will take place the first Saturday of the following month.

Regular attendance of those initiated is essential to attending the parties and trips or participating in the contests of the K. of T.

TEAR OFF THE COUPON AND PRESENT AT THE DOOR WITH YOUR NAME AND NUMBER.

APRIL 20. ~MARCH 23.~
Readings from Ralph Connor.

APRIL 13. ~MARCH 16.~
Dr. C. E. Hemingway, Speaker.
"A Boy's Relation to Himself and Other Boys, Past, Present and Future."

APRIL 6. ~MARCH 9.~
Stereopticon Pictures.

MAR. 30. ~MARCH 2.~
Dr. C. E. Hemingway, Speaker.
"A Boy's Relation to the Wild Animals of Cook County."

MAR. 23. ~FEBRUARY 23.~
No Meeting.

MAR. 16. ~FEBRUARY 16.~
Dr. C. E. Hemingway, Speaker.
"A Boy's Relation to Our Mountains and the Minerals Contained."

MAR. 9. ~FEBRUARY 9.~
Rev. E. V. Shayler, Speaker.
Subject, - - "My Trip Abroad."

MAR. 2. ~FEBRUARY 2.~
Dr. C. E. Hemingway, Speaker.

The Oak Park Club was organized in 1890 and met at several different locations in the village including the Hurlbut residence on North Boulevard. The Club was the scene of many gala parties including a "hobby" party held in 1915 at this North Boulevard location.

Members wore costumes that expressed their favorite occupations and, according to an account in the Oak Leaves, "Mrs. W.H. Hodge came as a cook wearing a gingham apron. Pinned to the apron was a sign, 'How to get and keep a husband,' and from her belt hung ladles, spoons, knives, eggbeaters, graters and other kitchen paraphernalia. Her hat was an inverted sieve."

There was no mention of what local suffragettes had to say about this display of erratic domesticity.

In 1923 the Oak Park Club erected this building at the southeast corner of Ontario and Oak Park Avenue, which became the center of all important social events including dances for Oak Park High School graduates and annual follies. In the seventies, dwindling membership forced the Club to disband and today the facility is being developed for condominiums.

The three-story building on the northwest corner of Lake Street and Marion, built in 1928 by Robert E. Nicholas (on the site of the old Steiner Building) to showcase his hardware, appliance and furniture emporium, has had a colorful commercial history.

Nicholas was a Canadian who came to Chicago around the turn of the century and eventually got a job at Stebbins Hardware in the city. In 1907 he and a friend opened a hardware store, Rogers and Nicholas, at 214 Lake Street (now 1015 Lake). Three years later the firm moved to the new building George Hemingway had just built on the northwest corner of Westgate and Marion, and in 1911 Nicholas bought out his partner. Business was so brisk his next move was to open a branch in the Scoville Block at Lake Street and Oak Park Avenue.

The twenties was a period of unparalleled building in the village and Nicholas saw an opportunity to supply new homeowners and apartment dwellers with furniture and appliances they would need. He extended his line of merchandise and moved his business to this new building at the northeast corner of Lake Street and Marion.

Shoppers at the Nicholas Company enjoyed amenities which included a children's playground on the fenced roof, underground parking, barber shop, lecture room for community meetings, practice room and driving net for golfers, and radio and victrola "try out" rooms.

However the following year The Fair, a Chicago department store, made an offer Nicholas could not refuse. After selling his business to the retailer he remained as manager of The Fair for a year and then left to pursue other interests.

In 1957. The Fair sold the building to Montgomery Ward, who occupied the property until 1975. The building remained unoccupied for a number of years while consideration for its use was given to several plans. Finally, in 1984 the property was purchased by Ken Tucker & Associates, developed into a vertical mini-mall with room for 40 shops on three levels, and renamed Park Square.

Photo courtesy of the Walker Company

Photo courtesy of Co-Operator Magazine

Photo courtesy of Co-Operator Magazine

Photo courtesy of Wednesday Journal

Opening day at the Lake Theatre, April 11, 1936. By the time this theatre opened the controversial question of whether Sunday movies should be allowed had been settled by a 1932 referendum in which voters finally agreed they should be shown.

During the twenties a hotly contested battle raged between the factions favoring and opposing Sunday movies in the village. The question appeared on the ballot in 1917, 1923 and 1925, and was defeated each time. This was due in large part to the impassioned rhetoric of opponents such as the Superintendent of District 97 who declared, "the wide open Sunday with theatres, pool rooms and dance halls will disorganize and destroy the mental, moral and physical efficiency of Oak Park children."

Even worse, it was feared Sunday movies would cause property values to plummet and taxes to soar. According to an article in the Oak Leaves, "New movie houses will increase taxes by reason of extra police protection and traffic hazards. Try and park within one quarter mile of any popular theatre on any evening. What will it be on Sunday? The hazard is great, the noise deafening, the confusion disasterous."

Opponents were fighting a losing battle, though, and in November, 1932 the proposition finally passed. Acceptance of Sunday movies reflected Oak Park's increased population with most new arrivals coming from Chicago. These people didn't fear Sunday movies and wouldn't accept the alleged evil in them.

The Depression also contributed to passage of the ordinance. Oak Park, like the rest of the nation, was suffering and in this pretelevision era villagers were anxious to forget their troubles if only for a few hours. The first movie to be shown on Sunday in Oak Park was aptly titled "A Successful Calamity," and starred George Arliss. *Photo Courtesy of Tivoli Enterprises*

The Warrington Opera House on the southeast corner of South Boulevard and Marion Street offered a matinee in this photo from the early twenties. During the twenties a series of traveling repertory companies stopped at the Warrington and entertained villagers with comedies, melodrama and mysteries. During intermissions salt water taffy was sold up and down the aisles. Later in the twenties the opera house made the transition to movie theatre.

The casual camaraderie villagers enjoy on summer Saturdays at the Farmer's Market, in the parking lot at Elmwood and Lake Street, is far different from the formal socializing that took place when this site was occupied by the Colonial Club, a social club that hosted events for the entire family.

The Club was the outgrowth of a Magazine Society started in 1894 by several couples on South Scoville. The meetings were held in homes, but in 1902 the Club was chartered and named the Colonial Club.

E. E. Roberts designed the new club house, appropriately with a design based on 18th century "colonial" New England styles. The three-story building contained a billiard room, bowling alleys, parlors, club rooms and a third floor ballroom.

Boys and girls were taught the social graces in Miss Mary Belle Ingram's dance classes; the men played cards or billiards, and bowled in a strictly masculine atmosphere; and the ladies met for lunch and cards in the parlor.

By 1931 the Depression had taken its toll and the Club was disbanded. In 1934 the building was acquired by the Pilgrim Congregational Church for use as a church house. The village acquired the property in 1971 and, after determining the cost of restoring the structure was prohibitive, razed it and developed the site as a parking lot.

Pilgrim Church later exercised its option to buy the property back and today rents a portion of it to the village for overnight parking, and to teachers at nearby Oak Park High School. The Farmer's Market also pays rent for use of the site every Saturday from June to October.

The Oak Park Post Office, built in 1906 on the northeast corner of Lake Street and Oak Park Avenue. In 1900 the Post Office was located at 105 North Marion. Delos Hull was postmaster and operated both his coal business and the post office out of the same building.

The facility grew so rapidly it soon ranked as first class, which entitled it to a building of its own. The government accepted Charles Scoville's price of $5,000 for the corner lot across the street from his late father's house.

There was strong opposition from the "west end" people, who had hoped to keep the new post office on Marion Street, but their haggling proved their undoing. Instead of uniting on a single site, they divided their efforts among half a dozen locations, while the Avenue people mounted a successful assult on Washington.

The new post office served the village until August, 1936 when the present post office at Kenilworth and Lake Street was completed. It was then demolished and the government sold the property to a developer who built the existing cluster of stores on the site.

OAK PAR
NO. 15
The America
PHOTO BY SINAY.

The Oak Park American Legion Post 15 Drum and Bugle Corps performed for all Veterans Day and Memorial Day celebrations in the village during the 1920s. They are pictured here in the ballroom of the Colonial club on Lake Street. *Photo courtesy of Les Paepke*

Colonel A.D. Rohm, grand marshal and Colonel Charles
Roth, chief of staff leading the Memorial Day parade in 1925.
They are followed by Colonel John Tape, Reverend F. R. Godol-
phin and Major W.F. Sims.

Pvt. Robbins (second from right), with his comrades at Camp Grant in 1917 prior to going overseas. Robbins served with the 139th Field Artillery Rainbow Division.

This 1927 photo taken at Camp Grant shows Private Robbins with his wife, Irene, and cousins, Jeanette, Georgia and Rowena Machimon of 729 South Oak Park Avenue.

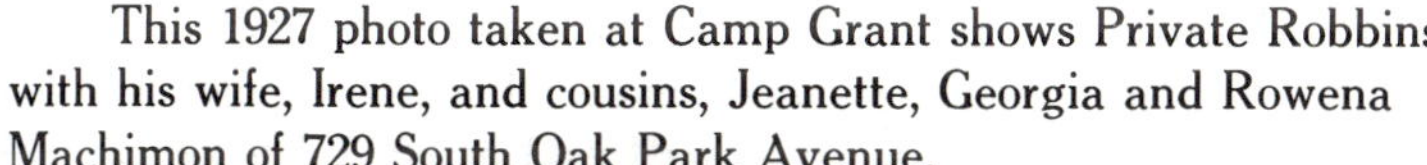

Private Edward Robbins in training at Camp Grant prior to being sent overseas.

"Pleasant Home," the Prairie Style mansion designed by George W. Maher in 1897 for John Farson. The 1972 Hasbrouck-Sprague Survey of Historic Architecture in Oak Park classifies Pleasant Home as early modern rectilinear with architecutral significance beyond the Chicago area. It is rated of national and international importance with a highly original architectural style.

The name of this stately home, which is listed on the National Register of Historic Places, is derived from its location on a 7-acre site at the corner of Pleasant Street and Home Avenue.

John Farson, millionaire banker and philanthropist who commissioned George Maher to build "Pleasant Home" in 1897. Although the property was surrounded by a steel fence it was never used as a barrier to isolate Farson from his neighbors. Instead the gate was left open so the property could be enjoyed by villagers at all times.

Farson attributed his business success to hard work and cheerfulness. "It is a great satisfaction to build up a business but money is not everything in the world. My home and my friends are my main source of happiness. There are so many rich men in this country who won't even smile. They don't get anything out of life. Be cheerful!"

Unlike other men of great wealth, Farson never became addicted to travel. He often expressed the sentiment that Oak Park was good enough for him. He had no country home and did not go away for the summer or the winter.

In 1897 the Prairie Style mansion known as "Pleasant Home" was designed by George W. Maher for John Farson, a prominent banker and philanthropist. Today the Park District of Oak Park has begun renovation of this stately house located at 217 S. Home.

The mansion presently serves as the home of the Senior Citizens' Center of Oak Park and the Historical Society of Oak Park and River Forest. It is also open for guided tours every Saturday and Sunday afternoon.

John Farson, whose trademark was a red necktie worn for all occasions, was a genial host who enjoyed sharing his home with his neighbors. From 1898 until his death in 1910, Pleasant Home, which encompasses almost a city block, was the scene of many festive lawn parties, balls, receptions, concerts and other social gatherings.

Farson had an extraordinary zest for life and for almost 20 years he intrigued, charmed and shocked the public. He was never accused of being dull and Oak Park newspapers were continually full of his activities.

Farson was an avid horseman who kept a stable full of horses in stalls built in the shape of a wheel. Friends and family could step into the center of this "wheel" to feed the horses sugar lumps without entering the stalls.

Even more revolutionary was the clock he installed on the exterior of the stables with chimes which pealed every quarter hour. At first neighbors objected, but as they became accustomed to the predictable peals the clock became a part of village life.

Within a few years, however, Farson succumbed to the lure of the auto and before long fine cars were parked in his stables instead of horses. As president of the Chicago Auto Club he favored an increase in driving speed and his chauffeur was frequently hauled into court for making village streets "look like crimson streaks" by exceeding the speed limit of eight miles an hour.

Anxiety for his wife's health prompted Farson's interest in a healthy outdoor regimen. He initiated a spartan lifestyle that included sleeping in the open air for much of the year. According to a local newspaper: "Millionaire banker fixes up a room on the roof and sleeps out of doors in all kinds of weather. He wears red pajamas."

The sleeping porch was on the roof above the kitchen and was provided with awnings and simple furnishings. When a reporter asked, "Do the neighbors peek?" Farson replied, "Oak Parkers are too well bred to peek."

Farson was fond of children, and when roller skating became the rage he championed the skater's cause against those who denounced the sport as a worse evil than the speeding auto, by opening his grounds for skating. He even took up the sport himself.

Scarcely a week went by that did not include an account of some social soiree hosted by the Farsons. Typical is a 1902 newspaper issue which contained two features on the couple. The first reported that a reception Mrs. Farson gave for 400 was "one of the most brilliant social events of the season," and the second was an account of a dinner John Farson gave for the officers of the Union League Club. "Guests were conveyed from the city by a special train provided by J. R. McCullough of the North Western Railroad."

John Farson died suddenly of a heart attack on January 18, 1910. Dr. James Herrick, an Oak Park native who achieved world prominence as the first physician to recognize coronary thrombosis, was called to treat the stricken man. Dr. Herrick, who had been studying similar cases, accurately diagnosed Farson's condition.

After Farson's death Dr. Herrick performed an autopsy which revealed he had suffered coronary thrombosis, the first officially diagnosed case of what we now call a heart attack. Farson's case history and Dr. Herrick's diagnosis were published in medical journals around the world. His death, like his life, had become public property.

The elaborately landscaped south garden of Pleasant Home. Following the death of John Farson in 1910 the property was sold to Herbert Mills, inventor of the slot machine. It remained in the Mills family until 1939 when it was sold to the Park District of Oak Park for $212,000, with the stipulation that the 7.1-acre estate be known as Mills Park and that the mansion become a community center to promote social, cultural and civic projects.

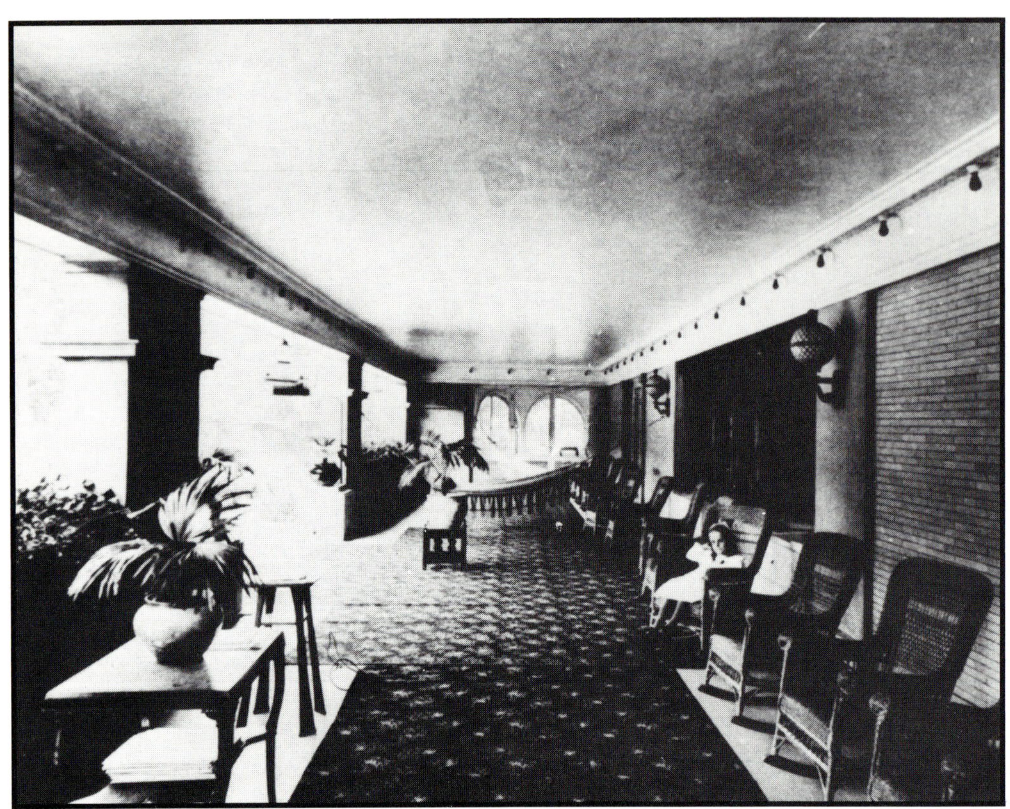

The front porch of Pleasant Home which runs the width of the house and can comfortably seat 100. This summer photo shows it filled with wicker furniture and hammocks for the comfort of guests. A red parrot made his home on the porch during the warm weather and squawked his greeting to all who entered.

Bedroom of the youngest Farson son, William, reveals a young man of eclectic taste who favored hunting, his collection of family photos, allegiance to Andover, and watching his weight on the elaborate scale in the corner.

The mahogany buffet, hanging cabinet, and dining room set are all original and were designed by Maher for this room. The architect successfully blended diverse influences and produced furniture with both the elegance of Renaissance tradition and the simplicity of the coming modern design, which stressed strength and mass, straight lines and plain surfaces.

The musician's alcove to the left was intended as an unobtrusive addition to the dining room where musicians could furnish background music for dinner guests.

In the library mahogany bookcases were built-in on three sides with carved lions' heads interspersed between the cases. Other decorative details include a green ceramic fireplace, a Tiffany window on an interior wall and dramatic rows of electric lights bordering the room.

HISTORIC CHANGES

The southwest corner of Oak Park Avenue and Lake Street, across from the home of James Scoville and later Scoville Park, has been an important village site for almost a hundred years.

The first photograph existing of a building on the site shows a small carpenter shop owned by J. P. Willing. Prior to that a company named Goetter and William, business unknown, occupied the property.

A large Queen Anne home belonging to the Blackstones, a prominent local family, was also built on this property. It is not known if both buildings occupied the site at the same time or if the Willing shop was razed to make room for the Blackstone home. At any rate, both buildings were demolished in 1908 when Charles Burton Scoville, son of James Scoville, commissioned Prairie School architect E. E. Roberts to design the Masonic Block.

In 1917 William Y. Gilmore, a traveling ribbon salesman with a home and family in Chicago, settled down and opened the Avenue Dry Goods in the store now occupied by J. B. Winberie restaurant. When his two sons finished college and joined the business in the early twenties he changed the name to William Y. Gilmore & Sons.

Through the years Gilmore's expanded and by 1959 the department store occupied the entire building. The Gilmores also remodeled so extensively that E. E. Roberts' original design was all but unrecognizable. For over 56 years six Gilmore men ran the Gilmore family business until the store closed in 1976.

The building remained unoccupied for years until the Industrial Fire & Casualty Company bought it in 1984, renamed it the Richard See Holson building, and restored it to its original 1908 appearance.

Today the building is the focal point of the Avenue Lake Plaza shopping district. As in years past, there is an exciting diversity of retail shops on the first floor while the upper floors are occupied by the home office of the Industrial Fire & Casualty Company and other businesses.

Carpenter shop of
J. P. Willing

The Blackstone Home

William Y. Gilmore Department Store in the fifties

Main entrance of the Richard See Holson Building, formerly
the Masonic Block. *Photo courtesy of Industrial Fire & Casualty
Company.*

For more than 80 years Oak Park Hospital has been offering skilled medical services to village residents. In 1987 the Wheaton Franciscan Systems, Inc. purchased the 350 bed hospital from the Sisters of Misericorde who had operated the hospital since it opened in 1907.

In 1904 the Oak Park Hospital Association, a nonprofit corporation, was formed to raise capital to build a hospital that would be under the jurisdiction of local physicians. Dr. J. W. Tope was chairman of the Association which included Dr. Clarence Hemingway, the father of Ernest Hemingway.

The site originally selected was the entire block bounded by Elmwood, Scoville, Augusta and Thomas which was priced at $14,000. When opponents agitated against the facility because of the perceived danger of infectious disease, the Association voted to dispose of its assets and disband.

Dr. Tope was determined there should be a hospital. He turned to the Sisters of Misericorde who had successfully established eight other hospitals, and they agreed to build a 90-bed hospital.

The building was dedicated on April 4, 1907. In less than two months 60 patients had been admitted and critics declared the hospital to be the finest of its kind in the country.

In 1906 ground was broken with Dr. Tope turning the first shovel. The building permit had been granted only when the application specified the hospital would not be used for treatment of infectious or contagious diseases.

The estimated cost of $125,000 was exceeded by $10,000 and the Sisters were forced to make an appeal to furnish the hospital. By this time Oak Parkers were willing to admit the new hospital was an asset to the village, so funds were quickly raised.

Through the years there have been many changes and additions to Oak Park Hospital. The largest was this six-story 240 bed addition built in 1955. Today Oak Park Hospital is one of 12 hospitals sponsored by the Wheaton Franciscans. The Hospital offers a full range of traditional acute care services plus a new Skilled Care Unit of 48 beds that is designed to provide the finest in hospice, skilled and respite care. *Photo courtesy of Oak Park Hospital.*

WEST SUBURBAN HOSPITAL

Although Oak Park Hospital had been opened in 1907 the need for a second hospital was apparent just a few years later. In 1911 the West Suburban Hospital Association composed of physicians from Oak Park and surrounding suburbs was formed.

Like Oak Park Hospital, the Association also experienced opposition from local residents when they tried to secure a site at Ontario and Austin Blvd. In 1911, however, the village issued the necessary permit and the original hospital was opened in 1914 to receive all cases except contagious and mental patients.

In 1982 a professional office building was added, and today West Suburban Hospital Medical Center has grown into a 372-bed, full service health and medical facility with a medical staff of more than 250 physicians supported by a clinical staff of 1,100.

The Center is the coordinating facility for paramedic service available by dialing Oak Park's emergency number, "911." It also offers a wide range of community health education programs, home health services, maternity services, family practice and internal medicine programs, Advantage Plan for seniors, Sick Bay for ill children of working parents, and many other specialized services ranging from cancer cure to coronary intensive care.

A nurses' training class at West Suburban in the 1920s. Enrollment in the hospital's school of nursing increased so rapidly that in 1926 a new building housing 200 nurses replaced the smaller facility built just ten years earlier.

West Suburban Hospital Medical Center, at Erie and Austin, is both a sophisticated medical facility and a valuable community resource offering the best in acute inpatient care, outpatient services and preventive programs. *Photo courtesy of West Suburban Hospital*

Off to summer scout camp at Lauderdale Lake, Wisconsin. True to their motto, "Be Prepared," these Oak Park Scouts in this 1920s photo each have a sleeping bag and other paraphernalia necessary for a two-week camping trip. Through the years village scouts have camped at various sites in Michigan and Wisconsin.

In 1947 the Thatcher Woods Area Council purchased Camp Shin Go Beek in Wisconsin. *Photo courtesy of Thatcher Wods Area Council*

CHAPTER IV

WAR
AND
PEACE

1930-1952

Few Oak Park families were unaffected by the Depression that followed the 1929 stock market crash. Like most of the country, thousands of villagers were unemployed and unable to pay their property taxes. In 1932 a reported 17.38 percent of the 1928 taxes were uncollected, 31.9 percent of the 1929 taxes went unpaid and a whopping 47.22 percent of the 1930 taxes failed to come in.

The effects of this eroding tax base were felt throughout the entire community. During the early thirties schools were forced to sell bonds to remain open and as late as 1936 the village was more than two and a half months behind in paying municipal employees.

Village officials struggled to maintain basic services and put villagers back to work with programs such as the Oak Park and River Forest Campaign for the Re-Employment of Men and Money. Under this plan both communities provided $117,537 to create 103 permanent and 445 temporary jobs for residents.

The Oak Park Public Works Department also put men to work on school buildings and grounds in the thirties. According to one record, 227 men were employed to remove undesirable trees and plant new ones, 82 men paved Madison Street, 30 painted the village hall, 35 were assigned to playground projects and 142 were given other Park District jobs.

In addition, the federal government, through the Works Progress Administration assisted the community by commissioning numerous WPA projects throughout the village that put many of the hundreds of unemployed to work paving streets, repairing lights and working on construction projects.

In the early thirties the Oak Park Welfare Association distributed food from the Red Cross to needy Oak Park families. When it became apparent that this was just one of many ongoing problems in the community, village leaders with the help of the Chamber of Commerce established the Community Chest of Oak Park and River Forest in 1935. The theme, "Give Once for All," became the rallying cry for the 1935 campaign in which over a thousand volunteers raised $100,000 that was divided among eleven agencies.

Oak Park had long been a solid Republican bastion but during the 1930s villagers began to vote Democratic in increasing numbers. In the 1932 presidential election Herbert Hoover received a majority of votes, but by 1936 Franklin Roosevelt and his offer of a New Deal for the unemployed were the clear winners.

The global tragedy of World War II did more to shape the history of the village between 1940 and 1950 than any local event. In 1940, as it became apparent that America was being drawn into the war, villagers began to reluctantly prepare for the inevitable.

Before the bombing of Pearl Harbor the U. S. had already drafted more than 1500 Oak Park men. In 1940 the Red Cross began a campaign to raise $75,000 in emergency funds for war defense at home and National Defense Postal Savings Stamps went on sale to help finance national defense preparedness.

Oak Park formed a civil defense unit for men between the ages of 35 and 50 to plan for the possibility of a war emergency in the village. Members of the Oak Park National Home Defense drilled regularly in the Beye school gym in preparation for an emergency.

There were other groups in the village, however, working just as diligently to keep the country out of war. They included America First, a nationwide group dedicated to isolationism, and the Keep America Out of War committee. All overt opposition to war preparedness ended on Sunday morning, December 7, 1941, when villagers were electrified by the news that the Japanese had bombed American ships at Pearl Harbor.

Village President Robert McMaster immediately called for every able-bodied citizen to serve in some capacity in the village's civilian defense committee. Volunteers signed up to serve on fire brigades, rescue squads and medical units, and to serve as air raid wardens, clerical workers, and in hundreds of other capacities. The village was divided into 48 districts for purposes of civil defense and an air raid warden assigned for every four blocks.

For four years the war dominated the life of every villager. Conservation and thrift were practiced to a degree unknown today. The lights went out in store display windows and theater marquees. Victory gardens flourished in every vacant lot and yard while village trucks made weekly curb pickups of wastepaper and tin cans. The Office of War Price and Rationing in the village hall became one of the busiest spots in town as villagers stood in line for everything from sugar registration to bicycle applications. A rubber salvage drive was organized and people received a penny a pound for scrap rubber. Fats were collected and converted into glycerin for explosives.

By the time the war ended, Oak Park, with a 1940 population of 66,015, had lost approximately 200 men. This figure included those killed and missing in action.

After the war 60 temporary housing units for returning veterans and their families were built on six sites in the villages located in parks and vacant lots. They were constructed of corrugated metal set on concrete slab foundations. The government provided the material, but the village landscaped the huts and the high school manual training classes built flower boxes to brighten their spartan design.

By 1952 the housing shortage had eased somewhat and village officials began to give notice to veterans to find other housing. Some of these emergency units were still occupied as late as 1954.

During the summer of 1947 some 500 parking meters were installed in three commercial areas. Motorists were given a grace period to become accustomed to them before police began issuing tickets. By 1949 the meters were paid for and producing a daily income of $160 which was used to purchase off-street parking.

In 1948, over the objections of farsighted citizens who urged the village to investigate the threat of Dutch elm disease, the board purchased 580 elm trees for $8,200. (That's $13.13 per tree or about what it later cost to cut off a branch of a diseased tree.)

The Cook County Highway Department completed its survey for the Oak Park and River Forest section of the Congress Expressway in September, 1948. The road was expected to be completed in five years but by 1951 only 40 percent of the necessary property had been acquired by the state.

The number of overpasses and stations for the new rapid

transit line in the middle of the expressway caused more delays. When the expressway was officially opened in October, 1960, Oak Park staged a giant civic celebration to express its profound relief that the project was finally finished.

The decade that began with the drafting of boys for World War II ended on an equally somber note as eligible young men were being inducted for the "police action" that was rapidly gaining momentum in Korea.

In the early fifties many parents kept their children close to home as a polio epidemic swept through the village. Between 1951 and 1953 an average of five or six cases were reported monthly in the community.

By 1954 the March of Dimes Foundation ran out of money to help victims and an extra fund drive was launched. Gamma Globin injections and a series of vaccine tests were begun in 1954. By 1956 Dr. Jonas Salk had perfected the Salk vaccine and, as a result, by the late fifties the scourge of polio had been eliminated.

The village board became the focal point of heated controversy and the source of acute embarrassment in the early fifties. Chicago newspapers detailed wrangling among trustees, unpaid village bills and accusations of patronage deals. Behind the headlines were severe financial problems, poor services, low morale and creeping decay that threatened Oak Park with blight and bankruptcy.

In 1951 the board, headed by President Glaesel, was split into two distinct and bitterly opposed factions. At some meetings the president and three trustees who sided with him would attend the board meetings and conduct business without the three minority trustees being present. On the occasions when all were present the president would cast the tiebreaking vote on controversial issues, giving his side the majority able to pass any legislation it wanted.

Innuendos, accusations and threats flew between the two groups some time before any evidence of real wrongdoing surfaced. The fact that the scandal broke in the Chicago daily papers chagrined many Oak Parkers and made some determined to do something about it.

While the grand jury met to pursue evidence of the link between Republican Committeeman Walter McCarron and the majority trustees, some citizens quietly investigated another form of government.

Since 1902, when Oak Park broke from Cicero Township to form a separate municipality, the community operated under the Illinois Cities and Villages Act as a village form of government consisting of a village board with an elected president and six trustees who all made and administered policy.

In 1951 the Illinois General Assembly passed legislation enabling residents to adopt the village manager form of government, in which a professionally trained public administrator would manage affairs according to policies set by the elected village board.

A group of nonpartisan citizens calling themselves the Village Manager Association collected enough signatures to put adoption of the village manager form of government on the ballot in a special referendum. In November, 1952 Oak Park residents resoundingly approved the village manager plan by a three to one margin.

The nonpartisan VMA then selected a slate of highly qualified candidates, and in the April, 1953 election the VMA aspirants won by a landslide. In 1957 elections the Republican slate was again backed by Committeeman McCarron, anxious to reassert control over village affairs; however, the Village Manager Association group again swept the field by a large majority.

View of South Oak Park Avenue from Garfield Street. This photo was taken on September 6, 1935, more than 20 years before the Congress Expressway dramatically altered this busy corner. Suburban Trust & Savings Bank then, as now, was on the northeast corner of Oak Park Avenue and Harrison and the popular Southern Theatre, 828 S. Oak Park, was directly north of the bank. *Photo courtesy of Suburban Trust & Savings Bank*

At about the same time that the Lake Street trains were being elevated, the trains that had run on the surface on Harrison Street since 1905 were being lowered and their tracks reconstructed to run parallel with auto traffic on the new Congress Expressway. Work began in April, 1957 on the Expressway to link Chicago with the western suburbs and was completed in October, 1960. *Photo courtesy of Suburban Trust & Savings*

An aerial view of the Oak Park Avenue Harrison Street business district in the 1930s. Then, as now, Suburban Bank & Trust at Oak Park Avenue and Harrison was the anchor for the shopping center while the Southern Theatre, two buildings to the north, was popular with both village youngsters and their parents during these bleak Depression years.

Plans for the Congress Expressway were not yet on the drawing board and the Harrison Street electric train tracks (right foreground) were still on the surface. *Photo courtesy of Suburban Trust & Savings Bank*

By 1962 the Lake Street "elevated" trains were actually elevated in Oak Park and all crossing gates like these at Ridgeland Avenue were removed. Work on this ambitious project began in 1951 when the village floated bonds to raise the tracks, thereby eliminating crossing gates which were dangerous as well as unsightly. *Photo courtesy of Village of Oak Park*

A 1930s view of Oak Park Avenue looking north from North Boulevard. by this time there were as many autos on the busy thoroughfare as there once were trees. The most striking change was the Avenue State Bank building, right foreground, built in 1921 on the site of the Public Service Company of Northern Illinois (formerly Chicago Suburban Water and Light Company) An A & P Grocery Store was in the space now occupied by Erik's Deli while Smithfield Foods, which would move to that spot in the forties, was located in the Masonic Block during this era. Palmer's Flowers has since moved to Roosevelt Road with the expansion of Avenue Bank. *Photo courtesy of Village of Oak Park*

Greenfield Park shortly after it was purchased in 1925 by the
Park District. It was later renamed Lindberg Park in honor of
Gustav A. Lindberg, the first superintendent of parks. Lindberg
was responsible for the design of all the parks purchased after
1920.

PARK DISTRICT OF OAK PARK

Although there was no lack of open space and natural beauty in Oak Park around the turn of the century, many farsighted citizens felt the need for a public park system, and a committee was appointed to consider various possibilities. In April, 1912 Oak Park voters overwhelmingly approved creation of a permanent park district. A board of five commissioners was appointed and lost no time issuing $200,000 in bonds for the purchase of the village's first three parks.

In what is probably the greatest real estate bargain in village history the board paid Charles Scoville $135,637 for what are today two of Oak Park's most heavily used parks: the "Old Cricket Grounds," later renamed Ridgeland Common, at Lake Street and Ridgeland Avenue; and the site of the Scoville estate at Lake Street and Oak Park Avenue, now known as Scoville Park.

That same year South Park, an area of 7.6 acres bounded by Garfield, Gunderson and East Avenue, was purchased for $27,940. (The site was later renamed Rehm Park in honor of Arthur D. Rehm, one of the first Park district commissioners.) In 1913 North Park, a 12.7 acre site at Ridgeland and Division, was purchased for $22,000. The name of this park was later changed to Taylor Park to honor the first president of the Park Board, Henry A. Taylor. All of these parks were designed by Jens Jensen, the internationally famed landscape architect.

Gustav A. Lindberg, the first superintendent of parks, designed all parks purchased after 1920 and revised Jensen's landscape work in Scoville Park to accommodate the War Memorial. Greenfield Park at LeMoyne Parkway, Greenfield and Marion, purchased in 1925, was later renamed in his honor.

The Park District continued to acquire land as it became available for use as playgrounds and parks. Today the District is custodian for a total of 26 sites scattered around the village ranging in size from a half-acre "tot lot" at Grove and Randloph to the 12-acre Taylor Park.

The first step toward the establishment of playgrounds in Oak Park was in 1916 when the village received $90,000 from Chicago in settlement for the property known as Town Hall Park, which was taken over by the city when Austin was annexed to Chicago.

The Village Board appointed a Small Parks Commission and authorized them to purchase parcels of land for use as playgrounds. A special election in 1918 gave the board power to issue $50,000 in bonds to augment this fund. The commission selected four sites for these new playgrounds. A competition was held for the design of the community center which would be the focal point of each neighborhood. One set of plans was submitted by Frank Lloyd Wright who had left Oak Park several years earlier and was already world-renowned for his innovative designs. It

was decided that Wright's "kinder-symphony" of designs were too impractical and expensive. Instead, the judges chose the work of John Van Bergen, one of Wright's students.

These community centers, which were originally named by neighborhood children, formally opened in 1921. By 1926, however, the playgrounds had been renamed after authors of famous children's books: Robert Louis Stevenson, Hans Christian Anderson, Lewis Carroll and Eugene Field. By 1931 three additional playgrounds and community centers had been added, named for Henry Wadsworth Longfellow, James Barrie and William H. Fox - the only center where a Park District commissoner took precedent over a famous author.

In 1929 a conservatory was built on the southwest corner of East Avenue and Garfield at a cost of $26,000. Here flowers and plants were raised for transplanting in parks throughout the village. Seasonal flowers shows also attracted thousands of visitors to the conservatory every year.

Throughout the Depression the Park District's community centers met the needs of not only children but of adults who suddenly found themselves unemployed and with a great deal of time on their hands. Game rooms were opened for young men, and centers were used for daytime meetings of adult groups and for evening social clubs. Free educational and recreational classes were also provided.

No village youngster could ever complain there was "nothing to do" with the imaginative activities offered by the Park District. Some of these included dancing, dramatics, bowling, fencing, cooking, acrobatics, sewing, aviation, sports, art, woodworking, playwriting, puppetry and much more. In this pretelevision era villagers did not wait to be entertained but instead took advantage of everything the Park District had to offer and entertained themselves.

During these early years Oak Park playgrounds were recognized nationally and achieved numerous recreational "firsts." They were pioneers in landscaping the grounds, they established the first aviation school for both girls and boys, and installed the first children's municipal theater in the country.

Field playground won second place award from the National Recreation Association in a nationwide contest of most beautiful grounds in the country. During the war Oak Park playgrounds won first place in a national scrap lumber contest sponsored by the U. S. government.

The Oak Park playground network was one of the first recreation systems to stress educational play, the result being that "graduates" of the Oak Park playgrounds later went on to win national honors in athletics, dramatics, crafts and dancing. *All photos courtesy of Park District of Oak Park*

Judging the doll buggy competition at Field playground in 1937 was no easy task. This annual event was held in all playgrounds and entrants were required to decorate their buggies and dress their favorite dolls at the playground to insure that the work was done by the child and not by an overzealous parent.

In March, 1926 the Park District organized a number of boys' bands which were trained by the playground director and furnished music for all playground events. These young musicians had just performed at a Memorial Day celebration in Scoville Park.

Throughout the year special holidays were marked by elaborate pageants. All playgrounds heralded the arrival of spring with
May Day pageants which were highlighted by the crowning of the
May Queen. This 1933 photo spotlights May Queen and her court
at Field playground.

Youngsters hard at work on their craft projects at Andersen
center in 1928. Recreational activities such as this were especially
important during the Depression when many families had little
money to spare for amusement.

Children enjoying the wading pool at Barrie playground in the thirties. These pools were an integral part of all playgrounds until the sixties when they were replaced by wading pools built at both Ridgeland Common and Rehm pool.

Proud artists display their crafts at Stevenson playground. Instruction for practical do-it-yourself projects such as woodworking, model furniture, embroidery and simple sewing were all popular during the thirties.

There she is, Miss Junior Playground of 1937! Baby bathing beauties pose at Andersen playground.

Summer activities at all centers culminated in August with a spectacular circus performance in which all youngsters who were enrolled in classes participated. This truck was loaded with young performers trying to drum up business for Andersen's circus in early August.

Relay races were just one of many popular athletic events that attracted children to village playgrounds in the thirties.

Father Robbin's Borrowed Time Club, begun in the 1870s for villagers who had reached the age of 'threescore years and ten,' continued into the 1930s and was the precursor of the numerous senior citizens groups that are so active in Oak Park today.

During the thirties the Park District provided a game room in their building at 620 Garfield, as well as this outdoor checkerboard in Scoville Park, which was for the exclusive use of members of the Borrowed Time Club. *Photo courtesy of Oak Park Public Library*

Lake Street looking west from Forest Avenue during the early forties. As the devastating ripple effects of the Depression began to recede, this two block business district became one of the busiest and most successful shopping centers in the Chicago metropolitan area.

Oak Park had one store for every 77 residents, according to the Federal Bureau of Foreign and Domestic Commerce in 1937. The Bureau accurately forecast the village would experience rapid business growth in the next few years. By the forties the Lake-Marion district was filled with shops and department stores having a reputation for fashion that attracted shoppers from Chicago and surrounding suburbs.

The economic struggles of the 1930s actually resulted in growth for the village. Federal figures showed that Oak Park residents were better fed and clothed than most U. S. citizens in mid-1937. *Photo courtesy of Tivoli Enterprises*

Oak Park's first bank, the Dunlop Brothers Bank, opened in this building on the northwest corner of Marion Street and North Boulevard in 1887. It had been organized just a year earlier by Simpson and Joseph Dunlop, two brothers who also built two massive Queen Anne homes side by side on North Kenilworth.

William Einfeldt, who later became president of Avenue State Bank, worked as a messenger in the bank which was absorbed by Oak Park Trust & Savings Bank in 1899.

First Bank of Oak Park has been serving Oak Park continually for more than 60 years on Madison Street at Austin Boulevard. In 1922 the neighborhood bank first known as Prairie State Bank opened a small facility at 11 W. Madison Street. Six years later the bank expanded to include the entire southwest corner of Madison and Austin.

During the Depression the bank never closed its doors or placed restrictions on its customers. Following World War II Prairie State Bank received a national charter and changed its name to Oak Park National Bank.

By the early seventies, however, it was apparent that the bank could better serve the needs of Oak Park and surrounding communities as a state chartered organization, and so the bank surrendered its national charter in favor of a state charter and became First Bank of Oak Park.

In 1973 the old offices and stores east of the bank were torn down and additional parking was made available; drive-in lanes were added three years later. The eighties brought extensive interior and exterior remodeling of First Bank including installation of a modern system of computer terminals which are visible signs of an ongoing commitment to the community and the customers it serves.

Oak Park National Bank in the forties after its expansion to include the entire southwest corner of Madison and Austin. The Bank has served as an anchor to the Madison Street business community since 1922. *Photo courtesy of First Bank of Oak Park*

An architect's sketch of Oak Park Trust & Savings on the northeast corner of Lake and Marion Streets.

The First Chicago Bank of Oak Park is a new name for Oak Park's oldest financial institution. On October 1, 1987 Oak Park Trust & Savings Bank, which was organized by Henry W. Austin, Jr. in 1892, became the First Chicago Bank of Oak Park, a subsidiary of First Chicago Corporation, which also owns the First National Bank of Chicago.

In 1892 Henry W. Austin opened the Oak Park State Bank in a small store at 204 Lake Street, just east of Marion, where it did business until 1899. In that year it absorbed the Dunlop Brothers Bank, moved into the Dunlop's building and changed its name to the Oak Park Trust & Savings Bank. In 1923 the savings institution built its present facility at Lake and Marion.

The first site of Avenue State Bank, Oak Park's second oldest financial institution, was a small one-room storefront at 126 N. Oak Park Avenue (in the space now occupied by Springer's).

In the summer of 1899 Willis Herrick organized the bank in his father's living room. by the time the bank opened on December 18, 1899 Herrick had named the following officers: C. E. Bolles, president; his father O. W. Herrick, vice president; and William Einfeldt, cashier.

Both his father and Charles Bolles were respected and influential members of the community (O. W. Herrick was Oak Park's first principal and the son-in-law of Joseph Kettlestrings) and Einfeldt had been actively engaged in banking in Oak Park since 1887 when he was a messenger for the Dunlop Brothers Bank.

Willis Herrick succeeded Bolles as president of Avenue State Bank and during his tenure the present Greek Revival brick building was built at 104 N. Oak Park Avenue, on the site of a water works built by James Scoville during the 1860s.

As a young boy Willis Herrick had gone skinny dipping on the same spot, which at that time was a pond, a remnant of an acient glacial water pool fed by deep artesian wells. Not many bank presidents can claim to have a desk over the exact spot where they went swimming as a boy!

First Colonial Bankshares Corporation purchased Avenue Bank & Trust Company in July, 1986 as one of six subsidiary banks that now make up the Avenue Bank Group. The following year Frederick D. Bernson was named president, C. Paul Johnson is chaiman of the board and Chief Executive Officer of the renamed Avenue Bank of Oak Park.

Lake Street looking east from Marion Street in the thirties, before the tracks were removed from the street and buses replaced streetcars. Lytton's had not yet built its own store east of the Lake Theatre and occupied the building now used by Baskins. *Photo courtesy of Oak Park Public Library*

There were no snowblowers or plows in February, 1939 to remove the 18 inches of snow that fell in Oak Park in six hours and brought all forms of transportation to a halt. These volunteers are clearing the street car tracks on Chicago Avenue near Marion Street. *Photo courtesy of Dino Dini*

Lake Street looking east from Harlem Avenue in the thirties, when owners of the cars parked on this busy thoroughfare could still keep them on the street overnight. At a 1939 board meeting trustees informally discussed an ordinance to ban parking on Oak Park streets from 2:00 a.m. until daybreak.

The trustees said they felt a man had no more right to park a car in the street after midnight than he had to stable a horse in the street. A local paper predicted a boom in garage building and renting if this ordinance were adopted. *Photo courtesy of Oak Park Public Library*

Traffic moved cautiously down Chicago Avenue near Marion Street when a 1939 blizzard blanketed Oak Park with the heaviest snow ever recorded to that time. Since all snow removal was done by hand and salt was not sprinkled on village streets, travel was always hazardous for several days after a major storm. *Photo courtesy of Dino Dini*

The crowded interior of Sweet's Pharmacy and Drug Store on the southeast corner of Marion and Lake Streets. Sweet bought the business in 1910 from L. M. Lovett, pioneer Oak Park druggist. In 1929 he moved his popular business to larger quarters half a block east at 1031 Lake Street.

Sweet's soda fountain was just as popular as the prescription counter. When he finally retired in 1946, Earl Sweet had filled 399,803 prescriptions and his soda jerks had probably concocted an equal number of sodas, sundaes and malts.

Retail building on the northwest corner of Oak Park Avenue and Harrison Street in the early twenties. In 1912 Suburban Trust & Savings was organized and opened its first facility in a ground floor store in this building with a capital of $100,000 and a surplus of $25,000.

William H. Rattenbury, founder of Suburban Trust & Savings Bank, had the foresight to recognize that families purchasing new homes would also require the services of a sound financial institution. Developers such as Thomas Hurlburt and Seward Gunderson who were building in the 'south prairie', south of Madison Street, provided many of the homes financed by Suburban Trust.

Millions in securities made the move across Oak Park Avenue on April 24, 1924 under the watchful eyes of Oak Park policemen as Suburban Trust & Savings Bank moved from this storefront at 835 S. Oak Park Avenue into its new building across the street.

SUBURBAN TRUST & SAVINGS BANK

Suburban Trust & Savings Bank, 840 S. Oak Park Avenue, a fixture in south Oak Park for more than 75 years. This community oriented, full-service bank pioneered in car and other types of installment loans and supported higher interest rates for savings.

Suburban Trust is actively involved in numerous civic and community organizations in the village and, in cooperation with the nonprofit Oak Park Development Corporation, provides assistance to new businesses that are either moving to Oak Park or expanding existing facilities. *All photos courtesy of Suburban Trust & Savings*

Main Lobby

Denis J. Daly, Chairman of the Board

A display window of the Walker Company at Oak Park Avenue and Lake Street during the National Washer and Ironer Week in October, 1938. The testimonial from a mother of twins and satisfied owner of a new Bendix washer is the focal point of the display. The mannequin dressed for a day at the office or shopping also helped convey the message that automatic washers freed women from the time-consuming drudgery of a day spent bending over a wringer washing machine.

Following the U. S. entry into World War II the manufacture of machines such as this Bendix model was halted for the duration of the war, and homemakers had to make do with reconditioned washing machines that Walkers sold for $27.50 to $39.50. *Photos courtesy of Village of Oak Park*

In 1932 these Universal gas ranges sold for less than a hundred dollars but even that price was too steep for many villagers during the Depression.

Christmas display of gifts "guaranteed to gladden the heart of any little girl" in the Walker Company window in the 1930s.

Interiors of two Oak Park homes remodeled by Austin
Brothers Construction Company in the thirties.

Area rugs offset shining hardwood floors; and the focal point
of every modern home was the large floor model radio where
family members gathered to hear such radio classics as "Amos
and Andy" and "Fibber McGee and Molly."

Instructor John Carleton with a group of senior members of the Park District's Aviation Club in the late thirties. After Pearl Harbor 30 young men already had their pilot's licenses and went immediately into either the Army Air Corps or the Air Force.

Lew Weimer, president of the club, was commissioned as a major in the Air Force. He volunteered for a dangerous mission over Germany where his plane was shot down and he was lost.

A group of Oak Park High School graduates who were trained in the Air Corps formed a squadron called "The Flying Huskies" and became known for their many daring raids behind German lines. *Photo courtesy of William Cassin*

OAK PARK AVIATION CLUB

Two senior members of the Oak Park Aviation Club celebrate important "firsts." Helen Rockwell was the first girl to solo in a Piper Cub and Neil Daniels (left) was the first member to solo at the age of 16.

Many girls who received flying instruction at the club later obtained civilian flying licenses. The girls' division of the club was sponsored by Amelia Earhart who declared that "the Oak Park Playgrounds took one of the most important steps in furthering aviation when they trained girls for flying." *Photo courtesy of William Cassin*

Senior members of the Aviation Club, sponsored by the Park District during the 1930's, receive instruction in the use of oxygen from instructor John Carleton. This photo was taken in the basement of a store on Lombard, south of Harrison Street, that the Park District rented for the club's use. *Photo courtesy of Park District of Oak Park*

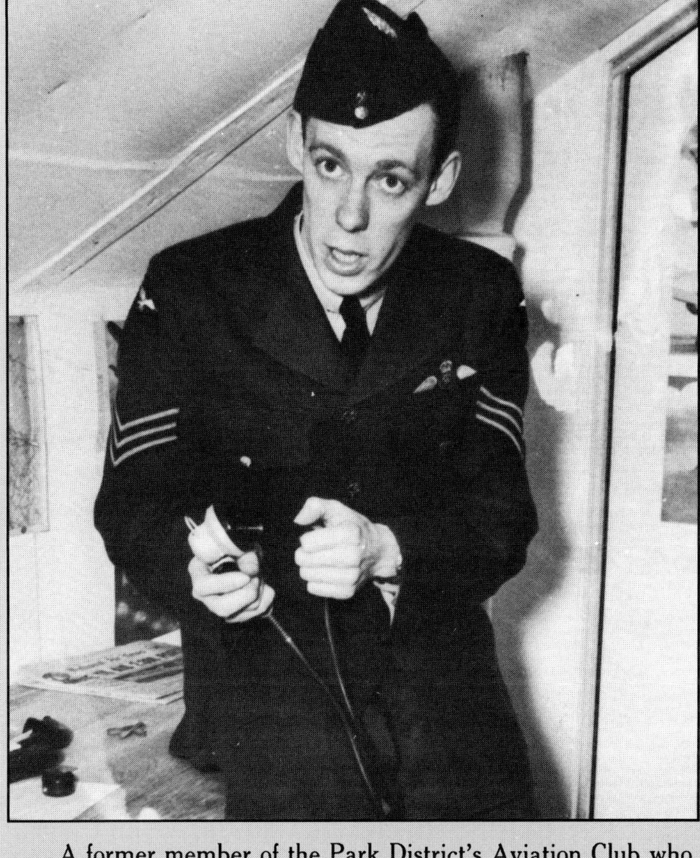

A former member of the Park District's Aviation Club who joined Britain's Royal Air Force before the U. S. entered World War II and returned later to Oak Park to talk to members. Once the U. S. was involved in the war, instructor Carleton regularly invited representatives from all branches of the service to address the students. *Photo courtesy of Park District of Oak Park*

Junior members of the Park District's Aviation Club confined their activities to making models of the planes they hoped one day to fly. William Cassin (left), and two other junior club members proudly display their models. Cassin, a lifelong Oak Parker, still resides in the village. *Photo courtesy of William Cassin*

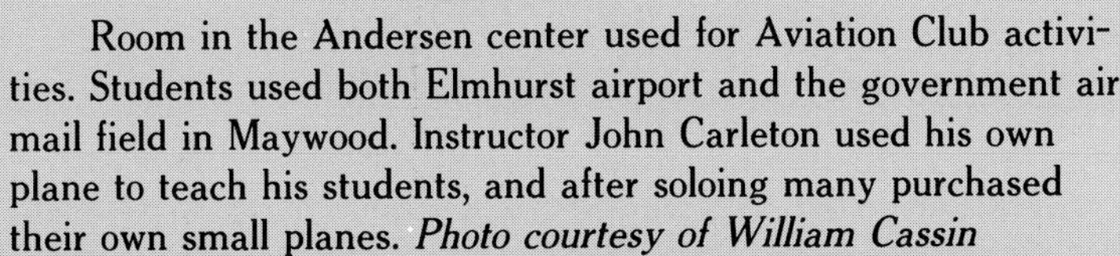

Room in the Andersen center used for Aviation Club activities. Students used both Elmhurst airport and the government air mail field in Maywood. Instructor John Carleton used his own plane to teach his students, and after soloing many purchased their own small planes. *Photo courtesy of William Cassin*

This "work in progress" photo taken in October, 1933 of Oak Park's new post office was supplied by contractors to government architects monitoring construction.

This facility replaced the old post office at the northeast corner of Lake Street and Oak Park Avenue which had served Oak Park since 1906. In 1931 the federal government purchased three parcels of land at Lake and Kenilworth for $175,000. The building cost $600,000 to construct. The architect was Charles E. White, a student of Frank Lloyd Wright. Wright's world-renowned masterpiece, Unity Temple, is located directly across the street.

The striking wall murals and art deco design of the interior makes the Oak Park Post Office one of the most attractive postal facilities in the country.

Charter members of the Oak Park Real Estate Board in the early twenties. Real estate activity was at a new high between 1906 and 1917 with most new homes built south of Madison Street. Between 300 to 400 building permits were issued annually until the pre-war peak was reached in 1915. After the war there was an even larger building boom in multi-unit apartments.

During this period 16 real estate brokers began to meet informally, looking for solutions to common problems. In 1917 the group was granted a charter from the National Association of Real Estate Boards. By the twenties, membership in the new Oak Park Real Estate Board had increased to 156 with most members involved in a variety of civic and charitable organizations.

During the Depression the Real Estate Board gave homeowners threatened with the loss of their homes the opportunity to join the Property Owners division of the board for protection of their homes.

The Oak Park Real Estate Board sued the Cook County tax assessor for illegal assessments of the wealthy, claiming the rich were not taxed sufficiently. A Supreme Court judge ruled in favor of the Realty Board and less affluent taxpayers were granted a 15 percent reduction in their taxes.

In 1956 the board changed its name to the Oak Park Board of Realtors and adopted the Multiple Listing Service, an idea first proposed in 1923. Today the Oak Park Board, located at 611 Madison Street, has approximately 400 active brokers and sales agents serving Oak Park, River Forest and Forest Park. *Photo courtesy of Oak Park Board of Realtors*

Lake Street looking east from Grove. The fountain in the foreground, built for the comfort of "horses, dogs and humans, " was designed by Richard Boch and Frank Lloyd Wright. It stood on this original site until 1969 when it was moved half a block east to Fountain Plaza at Oak Park Avenue and Lake Street, at the entrance to Scoville Park.

Over the years the fountain had fallen into disrepair but through the combined efforts of the village, the Park District and the generous support of citizens, over $20,000 was raised for its restoration and relocation. The move was made to coincide with the Frank Lloyd Wright Festival which marked the 100th anniversary of the architect's birth. *Photo courtesy of Oak Park Public Library*

Looking east on Lake Street from Oak Park Avenue in the late 1930s, before West Town buses replaced street cars operated by the Chicago and West Town Railways, Inc.

The ornamental iron lightpost in the left foreground was just one of 3,000 new lights added to the existing 1,000 lights when a new electric substation at Lombard Avenue and North Boulevard was dedicated in 1927. This new power plant, operated by the PSC, provided every street in the village with lighting. *Photo courtesy of Oak Park Public LIbrary*

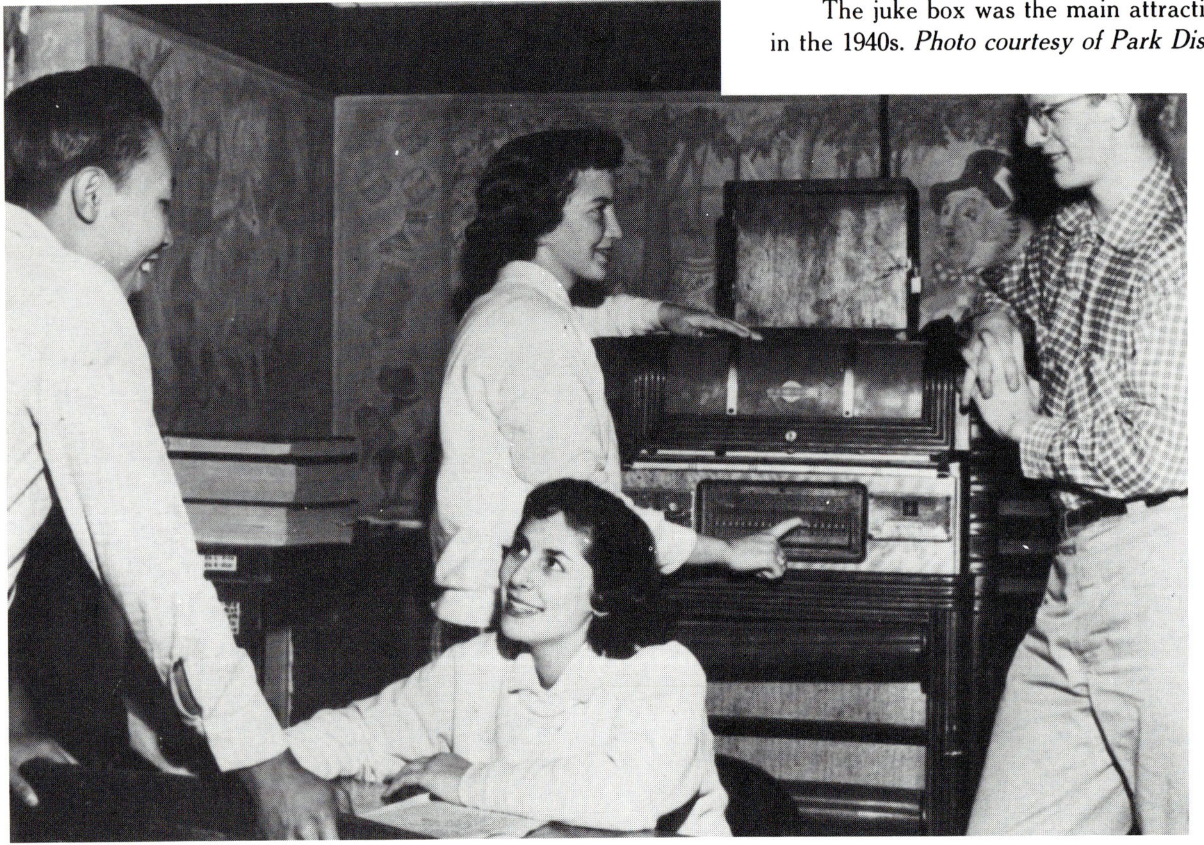

The juke box was the main attraction when teens gathered in the 1940s. *Photo courtesy of Park District of Oak Park.*

Bobbysoxers enjoying a Pepsi during a break at a high school sock hop in the 1940's. *Photo courtesy of Park District of Oak Park.*

CHAPTER V

THE CHALLENGE OF CHANGE

1953-1988

In the last four decades Oak Parkers have grappled with the same social, economic and political problems that have plagued the rest of the country. The process of dealing with these problems has revealed a society that is diverse and self-conscious but also united and strong enough to emerge in the late eighties as a leader and role model for other communities attempting to solve these same problems.

The first decade was a time of great tranquility, the calm before the storm. In the fifties Oak Park enjoyed great economic prosperity. Oak Park's 1954 retail sales were second only to Evanston in Cook County, and auto sales topped all other suburbs in the state. Oak Park schools underwent major expansions in population, facilities and budgets during this time. Ike was in the White House, mom was in the kitchen and dad was the chief breadwinner. Everything was as it should be.

Few villagers were prepared for the turmoil that was to engulf the country, and the community, during the sixties. The legacy of the sixties — the assasinations of a president and a civil rights leader, the explosion of inner city neighborhoods, the trauma of a undeclared war in Southeast Asia, turmoil on college campuses to protest that war, introduction of the drug culture into some Oak Park homes — made Oak Parkers stop and reassess their priorities and values.

The challenge of change gave rise to self-scrutiny and many villagers did not like what they saw. Two incidents during this period proved that Oak Park was not immune to the mounting racial tension which was threatening the nation. In the early fifties, the home of Percy Julian had been attacked. The incident was considered at the time to be the work of a hysterical outsider. When a black violinist was dismissed from the Oak Park-River Forest Symphony Orchestra in 1963, however, it became apparent that there was trouble brewing within the community.

With one eye on this incident and another on the resegregation underway in neighboring Austin, many Oak Parkers decided to deal constructively with impending change. Village president J. Russell Christiansen called a special meeting of the board to discuss the situation and seek remedial measures. As a result of the meeting, a Community Relations Commission was established for the purpose of ensuring a free and open Oak Park. That same year the Citizens Committee for Human Rights was organized.

On May 6, 1969, after months of heated public debate, the Oak Park trustees passed a landmark fair housing ordinance, one of 27 adopted by Chicago suburbs in that year. Although the ordinance marked the initiation of a comprehensive village program to achieve a stable and integrated community, it was opposed by a group of citizens who wanted to bring the question directly to the people in a referendum.

When this notion was defeated in the courts they formed two anti-ordinance parties and slated candidates for the 1969 election which was considered a referendum on the fair housing ordinance. The Village Managers Association slate (VMA), which supported the ordinance, won handily.

Oak Park entered the seventies with a population of 65,521. More than half of its adults were college educated with 37 percent of them in professional and managerial positions. The average family income was $16,126, almost $3,000 higher than all communities in the six collar counties surrounding Chicago.

As Oak Park continued to implement its pioneer ordinance and worked to achieve racial diversity, a new and sophisticated image of the community began to emerge. At the suggestion of the Community Relations Commission, the village hired a public relations firm to promote this positive, upbeat image.

During the Seventies Oak Park Elementary School District 97 was successfully reorganized in a positive effort to achieve racial balance in the schools. Following a 1974 policy statement by the Board of Education which concluded that individual Oak Park schools should reflect the racial composition of the district as a whole, the Committee for Tomorrow's Schools was formed. This joint task by parents and administration was for the purpose of recommending two or more plans for the maintenance of a racially balanced school system. Oak Parkers were committed to a voluntary reorganization as opposed to a forced restructuring mandated by the federal government.

After a year of intensive study, the committee recommended that the Board reorganize the district's ten schools. The two selected to be junior high schools were Emerson and Hawthorne (later Percy Julian) schools, both located in the geographic center of the village. Bussing would be provided only for junior high students in outer areas, and elementary students living in the junior high area. This reorganization plan was unanimously approved by the Board of Education, and was fully implemented in all District 97 schools by September 1977.

The seventies also brought an awareness of Oak Park's remarkable architectural heritage and Oak Parkers began to appreciate the diverse architectural mix of Queen Anne, Italianate and Prairie Style homes in the community. In 1970 a survey of historic buildings in the village was conducted and the result was "A Survey of Historic Architecture" which identified over 300 architecturally significant buildings.

In 1974, in the hope of luring back shoppers and retailers who had abandoned the Lake-Marion-Harlem shopping district in favor of regional shopping malls, village trustees turned the shopping district into a landscaped pedestrian mall. After 14 years however, and several futile attempts to revive sagging revenues, the present board has voted to reopen Lake Street to auto traffic in an attempt to revitalize this once thriving shopping district.

In 1984 trustees took a stand against handgun violence when they passed an ordinance that forbade private ownership of handguns within the community. Many villagers felt a personal involvement in the issue following the 1983 death of James Piszczor, an Oak Park lawyer who was shot and killed by a handgun in a Chicago courtroom (his wife Maureen later became an active participant in the Oak Park Citizen's Committee for Handgun Control). The ordinance was modeled after a similar ordinance adopted in 1981 by the village of Morton Grove. Debate over this controversial law (which was almost without precedent) raged both before and after its passage and thrust the village into the national spotlight.

The 1985 election marked another milestone in Oak Park history when three candidates representing Citizens Active for a Responsible Electorate (C.A.R.E.), a new political party that had been formed just 14 months earlier, were elected village trustees — thus ending the unbroken 32-year winning streak of the Village Managers Association, which had successfully slated candidates for village office since 1953.

Today Oak Park is considered by many as a successful living laboratory of social change and the community enjoys a national reputation as a model for other communities dealing with the same problems. The village has been the subject of several network shows and has been featured in numerous national publications including the *New York Times, The Wall Street Journal, Newsweek,* and *The National Observer.*

During the fifties millions of kids and adults began to exercise hip joints and muscles they never knew existed before the hula hoop craze swept the nation. These Oak Park youngsters could have given Elvis a few pointers in hip gyrations as they practiced in a Park District community center during the fifties. *Photo courtesy Park District of Oak Park.*

Football was just as important in Oak Park in the fifties as it is today. This photo was taken in October, 1951 before a game between a team sponsored by Oak Park Playgrounds and a team from Waukegan. The outcome is unknown, but if enthusiasm counted for anything the Oak Park team was the winner. *Photo courtesy of Oak Leaves.*

FENWICK HIGH SCHOOL

For almost 60 years Fenwick High School for boys has been a landmark on Washington Boulevard in Oak Park. In September of 1929 twelve Dominicans led by Father Leo Gainor, O. P. opened the handsome granite and limestone building to nearly 200 boys from Oak Park and the west side of Chicago, just a month before the beginning of the Great Depression.

Fenwick, however, survived the Depression and continued to grow. In 1945 a Building Fund was created. In 1948 the Priory was completed and in 1953 the west wing which houses a cafeteria, auditorium and nine additional classrooms was added.

Academic excellence has always been a Fenwick hallmark. From 1975 to the present, 30 percent of all Fenwick students have been Illinois State Scholars. From 1980 to date, 10 percent of each senior class have been National Merit Scholars, and in 1983 Fenwick was selected as one of the top 60 private schools in the nation by the U.S. Department of Education.

Today's Fenwick Friars continue in the tradition of athletic excellence established by legendary coach Tony Lawless who came to the school when it opened in 1929. Lawless coached basketball until 1947 and football until 1956, and continued as Athletic Director until his death in 1976.

Lawless led Fenwick to an impressive football record of 180 wins, 47 losses and 7 ties. He won 14 sectional titles, 5 Chicago Catholic League crowns and two City Championships in his 26 years at Friar head coach. *All photos courtesy of Fenwick High School.*

Fenwick High School occupies the entire south side of Washington Blvd. between East Avenue and Scoville. The college preparatory school for boys was named in honor of the first bishop of Cincinnati, Edward Dominic Fenwick, a Friar who established the Dominican order in the United States.

In 1928 George Cardinal Mundelein invited the Dominican
Fathers to build a new high school that would serve Chicago's
west side and the rapidly growing suburbs. On August 13, 1928
the cornerstone bearing the shield of the Dominican Order was
set in place by the Rev. Raymond Meahger, O. P., Provincial. Father Leo Gainor, O. P., the school's first principal, is on the left of
the cornerstone.

A lighter moment in one of Father Joseph I. Hren's Latin
classes. Father Hren has taught Latin and kept Fenwick students
interested in the Classics since 1949.

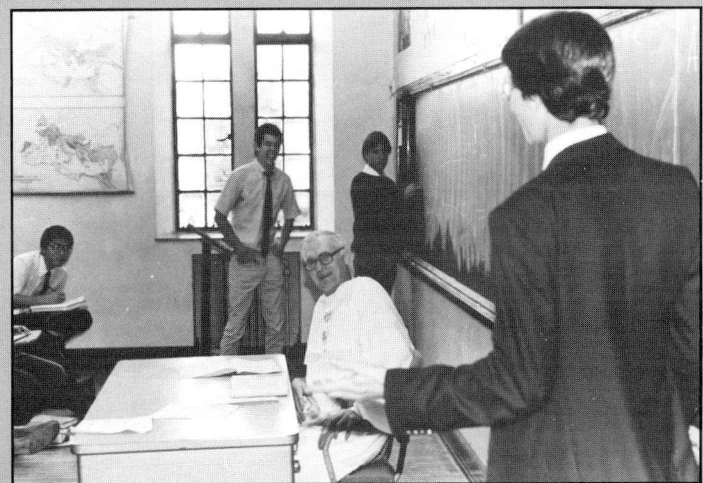

Fenwick - 1982-83 Varsity Football Team

Tony Lawless, who had the longest tenure of any man in the Chicago Catholic League's 70-year history, came to Fenwick when the school opened in 1929.

In basketball, legendary coach Tony Lawless led the Friars to the Illinois Catholic Championship in 1935. In 1937 they were named National Catholic Basketball Champions. Later, under coach Bill Shay, Fenwick won two City Championship, in 1950 and 1968.

The Fenwick Friars had a perfect 10-0 season in 1962. They took the Catholic League crown and went on to claim the City Championship with a 40-0 thrashing of the Schurz Bulldogs before 95,000 at Soldier Field.

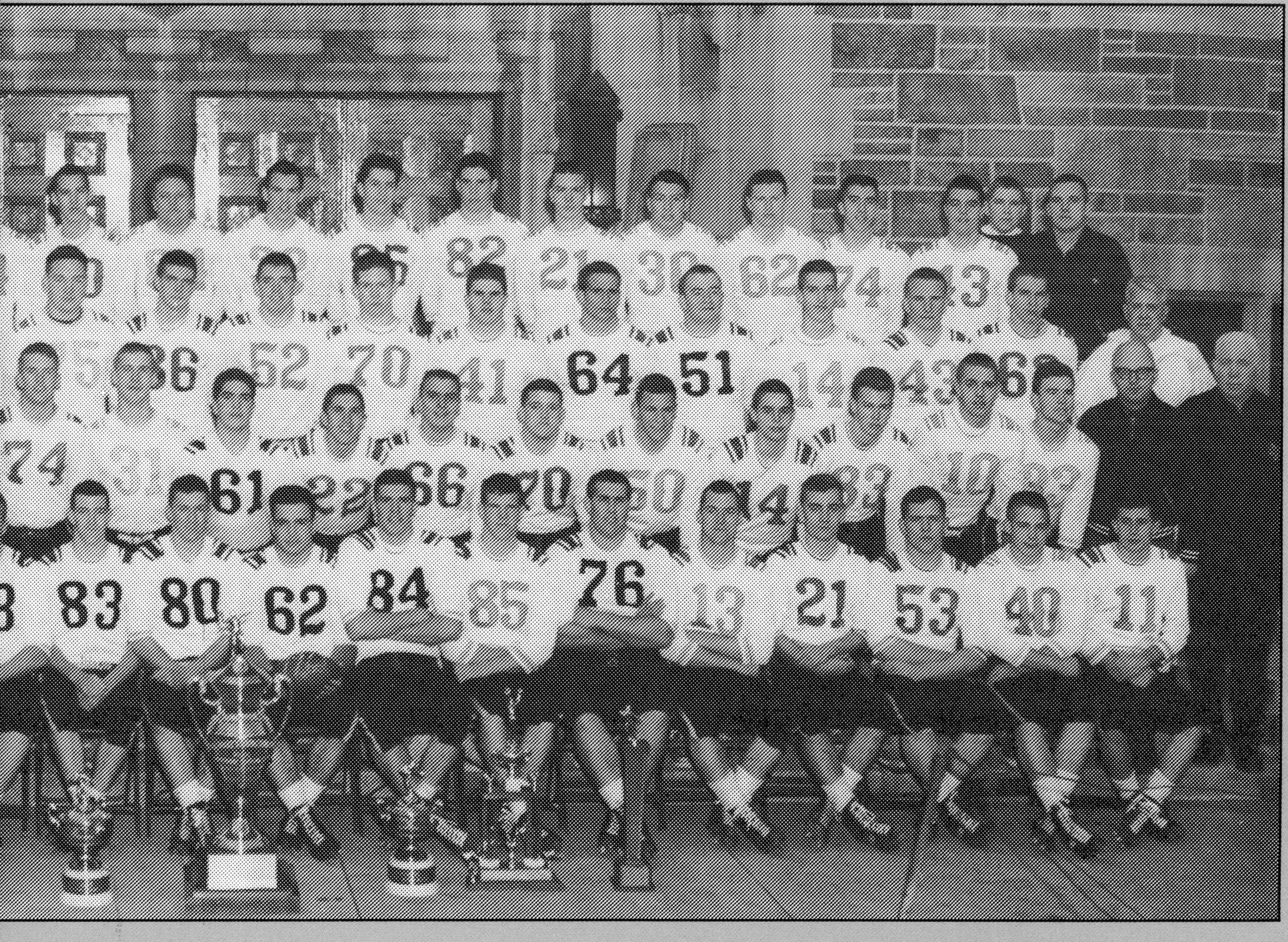

The food store and radio repair shop on the southwest corner of Lombard and Harrison, and the barber shop on the northwest corner are all long gone. *Photo courtesy of Village of Oak Park*

Village sanitation truck in 1957, when Oak Park's combustible waste was burned in an incineration plant at North Blvd. near East Avenue. At that time two trucks were used to collect garbage, one for combustible waste that was burned at the plant and the other for noncombustible waste, such as glass and metal, which was trucked to land fills.

In 1960 the plant, which did not meet current EPA standards, was razed and all village waste was combined and disposed of in land fills. At that time no one gave serious thought to the possibility that land fills would eventually reach the limits of their capacity and be forced to close — leaving municipalities scrambling for alternate means to dispose of solid waste.

Today the danger land fills pose to the environment is widely recognized, as is the need for (and profit in) recycling solid waste. The Oak Park Public Works Dept., working in cooperation with the Environmental & Energy Commission, has initiated a pilot recycling program in which homeowners in selected areas are asked to place all cans, glass and newspapers in recycling containers provided by the village.

These recycleable materials are picked up by a separate truck and brought to a transfer station where they are separated and sent to several different manufacturers for reprocessing. It is hoped that this program will provide a solution to the serious problems of the diminishing number of available land fills and the increased danger to the environment by hazardous household waste. *Photo courtesy of Village of Oak Park*

Parents were actively involved in all playground programs and also used the centers for their own social activities. These women are planning a mothers club card party at Carroll center in April, 1953. *Photos courtesy of Park District of Oak Park*

With the exception of football, girls participated in the same sports programs and activities as boys. These girls formed a softball team at Barrie Playground in the early fifties.

In 1953 the stereotype of the girls as tomorrow's homemaker was clearly defined. No boys were enrolled in this cooking class held at a neighborhood recreation center.

Lake Street looking west from Forest Avenue in 1974, just before the Lake-Marion-Harlem shopping district was closed to traffic and enclosed in a mall. In December of 1976 Oak Park Federal Savings (left) became Great American Federal Savings.

For almost ten years this makeshift wooden fence (left foreground surrounded the "Stankus Hole" named for the developer who tried, and failed, to build two 57-story towers on this 3-acre property which is now the site of 100 Forest Place.

Although the project was later scaled down to 37 stories a combination of financial problems, zoning obstacles and broad-based community opposition finally forced the developer to abandon the project.

Lowell School, built in 1924 on the corner of Lake Street and Forest Avenue to replace the old Central School. It was demolished in 1972 when the site was targeted for two 57-story residential towers. Those plans did not materialize and in 1986 the 100 Forest Place development was built on the property. In its 50-year history Lowell School served many purposes, including a library while the old Scoville Institute was razed and the present library was being built.

The 144-unit tower of 100 Forest Place was designed in the "Chicago School" tradition, with windows that go around corners and bays to let in maximum light. Corner windows and projecting bays provide sweeping views of nearby parks, forest preserves and the Chicago skyline.

100 Forest Place is built on the site of Central School, the village's first permanent school. In the twenties this pioneer building was replaced by Lowell School.

This $18.8 million project was financed through tax-exempt bonds issued with four Savings & Loan Network shareholders acting as surety. This was one of the first multiple savings and loan credit enhanced, tax-exempt revenue bond transactions in the U. S. *Photo courtesy of RESCORP Development, Inc.*

100 Forest Place, a luxury residential and retail rental development located on a 3.3 acre parcel of land at Lake Street and Forest Avenue. This "village within a village" which was completed in December, 1986 is a complex of 234 apartments in a variety of styles. Dominating the site is the 15-story tower apartment on its own landscaped park, with a 3-level parking garage, partially underground, to tuck 234 cars out of sight. Around the periphery are ingeniously designed two-story townhouses, piggybacked on top of garden level apartments. The garden apartments face the street and have their own walled patios. The duplexes on a raised plaza level have a private outdoor area and are reached via the interior landscaped park.

Developers of 100 Forest Place are Forest Place Associates, an Illinois Limited Partnership with RESCORP Development, Inc., and The National Housing Partnership as general and limited partners. *Photo courtesy of RESCORP Development, Inc.*

Students at Longfellow School opening a box sent to them from their pen pals at a school in Nepal, whose school had been built with funds provided by the Oak Park Council on International Affairs.

The Council was formed in the 1930s to study world cultures and problems. In 1964 members began to participate in the School-to-School Partnership Program which is monitored by Peace Corp volunteers who live and work in the area. Today this program is known as the Peace Corp Partnership Program.

By 1988 the project had funded over 107 schools and leads the nation in the number of schools built and renovated. The average cost for each school is about $1,000.00.

With the support of their American partners, citizens in target communities in developing countries initiate and plan the new school. At least 25 percent of the total project cost comes from the local community as well as all land, labor and locally available materials. *Photo courtesy of Wednesday Journal*

These young players know that choosing the most advantageous batting order is the most important part of the game. *Photo courtesy of Park District of Oak Park*

Bob Lagergren, former president of Suburban Trust & Savings Bank, surrounded by the players of the boys' baseball team which the bank sponsored in the early sixties. *Photo courtesy of Park District of Oak Park*

Charles Schultz and Katherine Falk, king and queen of the 1987 Senior's Senior Prom at the Oak Park Arms. The residents of this retirement community have as much fun planning this annual event as their younger counterparts at the local high schools have preparing for their prom.

Since 1980, residents of the Oak Park Arms have contributed toward a college scholarship which is awarded the evening of the prom to a deserving senior at Oak Park and River Forest High School. *Photo courtesy of Wednesday Journal*

For twenty years the Park District of Oak Park has provided recreation in the streets for village youngsters, with a trailer filled with recreation equipment that visits different blocks, by request on weekdays during the summer months.

This scene from a 1970 photo can be duplicated today throughout the community as recreation leaders plan games and arts and crafts activities for neighborhood children. *Photo courtesy of Park District of Oak Park*

REHABING OAK PARK

The 1980 census figures reveal that out of 22,620 households in the village 10,502 are single-family homes and the remaining 12,058 units are renter occupied. Most of these apartments were built in the twenties and range from modest two-story flats to large 45-unit courtyard apartments.

But, unlike a vintage bottle of wine, many of these buildings did not improve with age. Irresponsible owners and tenants, minimum or no maintenance, and failure to modernize all took their toll over the next half century. By the sixties, many apartments had gone beyond the point of simply requiring deferred maintenance and were in need of major renovation.

In 1973 the Oak Park village board addressed this problem by creating a $3 million Housing Bond fund financed by the sale of general obligation bonds. These private funds, which provided low interest rehab loans, assisted landlords to improve almost 1,000 rental units in the seventies. When these funds were depleted the board reinvested in the program by floating $3 million in bonds in 1982 and $2.5 million in 1985.

Oak Park's innovative approach to maintaining multi-family buildings has been copied throughout the country by communities facing similar problems. For example, in addition to receiving low interest rehab loans, landlords who agree to rent their buildings according to the economic and racial diversity guidelines set by the village are also eligible for Diversity Assurance Grants which do not have to be repaid.

If landlord are not interested in renovating multi-unit buildings they are often purchased and rehabilited by the Oak Park Residence Corporation using Community Development funds, Oak Park Housing Bonds and funding from other sources.

The Residence Corporation, which has a proven record of turning derelict property into showcase apartments, purchases property the Oak Park Housing Department has designated as targets for rehabilitation. Once this rehab is accomplished there is a five year holding period in which the Residence Corporation continues to manage the property.

The purpose of this postponement is to give the market value of the apartment building a chance to catch up with the estimated value of the property. When this occurs it is a trigger to sell the building and roll the profits back into still another building. Another reason for the delay is to promote the village's policy of racial diversity by creating white demand in an overimproved building where the majority of tenants are minorities.

The village of Oak Park also recognizes the importance of maintaining single-family homes and offers homeowners assistance in every aspect of home improvement. The Community Development Department currently offers three different federally funded housing rehabilitation assistance programs for one to four-unit owner-occupied properties that provide financial incentives to eligible low and moderate income homeowners.

The Oak Park Historic Preservation Commission also offers courses and printed materials on home restoration, and assists homeowners living withing the boundaries of both the Frank Lloyd Wright/Prairie School of Architecture Historic District and the Ridgeland/Oak Park Historic District to obtain property tax freezes, federal tax credits and state grants if they are restoring buildings which contribute to the character of either District.

Finally, the Oak Park Community Design Commission, established in 1973 to enhance the aesthetic quality of life in the village, offers homeowners guidelines for home rehabilitation and promotes high levels of maintenance of Oak Park homes.

Darnell Hawkins and Charlie Rife take a break from their renovation work on a home on S. Maple. *Photo courtesy of Oak Leaves*

Nancy Dominowski, Oak Park building inspector, examines the exterior of a single-family home in the 1000 block of S. Elmwood for housing code violations as part of the Neighborhood Walk Program. *Photo courtesy of Oak Leaves*

This Queen Anne bungalow at 1122 Ontario is believed to be the oldest home still standing in Oak Park. The age of homes built prior to 1902 is difficult to determine because all records remained with Cicero Township after the village broke away from the Township and established an independent government in that year. These housing records were subsequently lost in a fire.

Pleasant Circle, a 19-unit building at 302-304 N. Austin Blvd., is just one of many large multi-unit buildings that have been acquired and rehabbed by the Oak Park Residence Corporation, a quasi-official branch of village government using Community Development funds and Oak Park Housing Bonds. *Photo courtesy of Oak Leaves*

Joe Borges, owner of Harrison West, a 31-unit building at 27-35 W. Harrison Street, washes third floor windows after the completion of rehab work on the building in 1987 with the use of Housing Bond funds.

This Victorian home at 303 S. Humphrey is in the Ridgeland/Oak Park Historic District. *Photo courtesy of Oak Leaves*

This recently rehabbed Queen Anne home at 139 S. Grove Avenue is typical of 1 to 4-unit properties that are eligible for federally funded housing rehab assistance through the Community Development Department. *Photo courtesy of Wednesday Journal*

Geraldine McCullough, a nationally acclaimed artist and sculptor and a faculty member of Rosary Colege for the past 20 years, is an Oak Park resident whose home and studio is in an imposing four-story building at 117 S. Lombard, built by the CTA in 1903 for use as a generating station for their trains.

McCullough's work, which is displayed around the country, includes "Pathfinder" in the court of the Oak Park Village Hall and "Stopping by Woods on a Snowy Evening," a life size bronze statue of Dr. Martin Luther King, Jr. which was commissioned by Illinois Governor James Thompson and placed in the rotunda of the capitol in Springfield in 1988. *Photo courtesy of Wednesday Journal*

The generating station which now serves as a home and studio for Geraldine McCullough, shown shortly after it was built in 1903. When the CTA began purchasing electricity from Commonwealth Edison the building was used only for storage and was finally abandoned in 1967.

McCullough and her husband Lester purchased the property and spent several years replacing 127 windows, removing 6 layers of paint, and completing other necessary and major repairs. The 3-story studio is the ideal place for McCullough to work on her sculptures, which weigh several thousand pounds each. It is the size of a football field, filled with heavy welding and cutting equipment, and with a loading dock in back to facilitate moving these massive pieces.

ASCENSION

Ascension School 2nd grade teacher Sister Bernadette checks the work of Peter Gibbons. Today the parochial school at East Ave. and Van Buren Street has an enrollment of 375 students. *Photo courtesy of Wednesday Journal*

In addition to classes for kindergarten through 8th grade, Ascension School has also met the demand for day care for younger children by offering programs for 3 and 4-year olds. Teacher Julie Roggi pretends to be a ticket agent for her 4-year-old students.

ST. CATHERINE/ST. LUCY

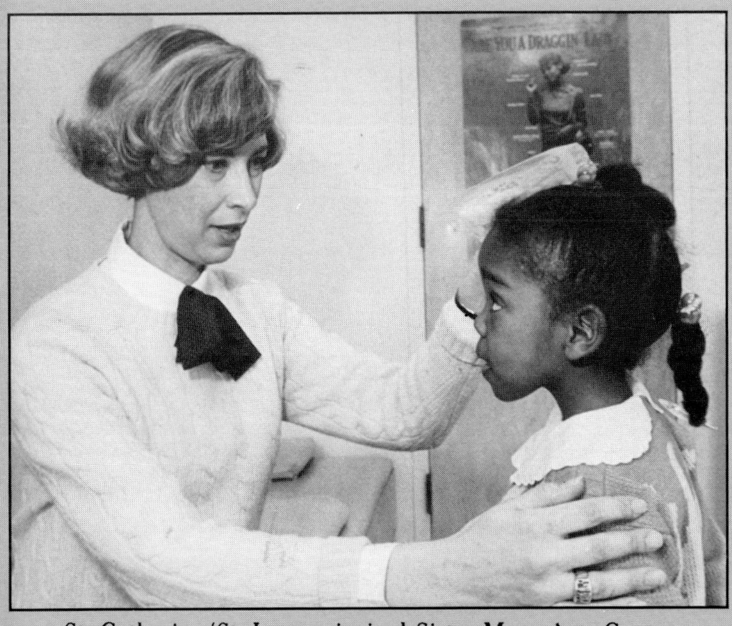

St. Catherine/St. Lucy principal Sister Mary Ann Cypser applies ice to the head of Lashaun Wilson. St. Catherine grade school at Washington and Humphrey opened in 1910. In 1974 the school merged with St. Lucy grade school in Chicago and today the school primarily serves Chicago students. *Photos courtesy of Wednesday Journal*

St. Catherine/St. Lucy 8th grader Chris Blunt works a math program the school computer. The school today has an enrollment of 346 students in preschool through 8th grade.

St. Edmund's offers a program for 3-year-olds two days a week, and a regular full-time curriculum for pre-kindergarten through 8th grade.

These four students represent the three grade levels: primary, middle and junior high. *Photo courtesy of St. Edmunds*

St. Edmund 2nd graders Josh Rusinak and Judi Borg work on science project "Solar Trek" for Science Expo '87. The school at Oak Park Ave. and Pleasant was started in 1912 and has a present enrollment of 200 students. *Photo courtesy of Wednesday Journal*

ST. GILES

Mrs. Margaret Stewart gives last minute instructions to her 5th grade class at St. Giles before a math test. The school at 1044 N. Linden opened in 1927. *Photo courtesy of St. Giles*

Mr. Edward Patricks, junior high science teacher at St. Giles, explains an assignment to a student. St. Giles has an enrollment of 486 students which come from both Oak Park and Chicago.

High school students riding in the Lake-Marion-Harlem Association's float in the 1972 community Christmas parade sponsored by the Oak Park and River Forest Chamber of Commerce. *Photo courtesy of Oak Park and River Forest Chamber of Commerce*

The atrium of The Oaks, a once prestigious 129-unit luxury apartment at 328 N. Austin Blvd. which was transformed into a 76-unit apartment for the elderly and handicapped through the joint efforts of the Oak Park Housing Authority and Oak Park Residence Corporation.

In 1976 the Housing Authority purchased the building which, at that time, was occupied primarily by squatters and was in completely derelict condition. The Residence Corporation received a $4 million grant from HUD to purchase the building from the Housing Authority and remodel it for senior citizen congregate housing.

The former Chateau Hotel was actually two separate units sharing a common facade. The buildings were gutted, the space between them enclosed in an atrium and 76 new apartments were created, each containing all the amenities that make life easier for the elderly and handicapped.

In 1981 the American Institute of Architects recognized the unique design of this rehab project by bestowing one of its prestigious Honors Awards on the architectural firm of Nagle, Hartray & Associates, Ltd., designer of The Oaks.

Today the Residence Corporation manages this building which provides subsidized rent for eligible tenants, who pay no more than a quarter of their total income for rent. *Photo courtesy of Oak Leaves*

An important element in the renaissance of village housing has been the Oak Park Housing Authority, a municipal agency that was chartered in 1946 but remained largely inactive until the late sixties; and its agent, the not-for-profit Oak Park Residence Corporation, created in 1966 to upgrade the quality of the housing stock in Oak Park through the acquisition, rehabilitation and management of multi-unit buildings.

The Oak Park Housing Authority is charged with administering the Section 8 Housing Assistance Program for low and moderate income tenants. In 1975 the Housing Authority built Mills Park Tower, a 199-unit building at 1025 Pleasant Place, with the help of federal funds. Today the agency manages this high rise which provides subsidized housing for low and moderate income elderly. *Photo courtesy of Oak Leaves*

Parkway trees still form a graceful arch today despite a debilitating attack of Dutch Elm Disease on village trees in the late sixties and seventies, when elms made up 95 percent of the village's tree population.

Oak Park has always been renowned for its beautiful trees. Joseph Kettlestrings and James Scoville were just two notables who were attracted to the area because of the majestic native oaks.

During the Depression 7,000 undesirable parkway trees such as cottonwoods and catalphs were removed with labor supplied by the WPA and thousands of new trees, including a large number of elms, were planted. *Photo courtesy of Wednesday Journal*

The sight of a forestry crew like this one pulling down a diseased elm in front of 325 S. Home Ave. was familiar in the mid-seventies, when as many as 1,500 diseased elms were lost each year. The worst year was 1974 when Oak Park lost 7 percent of its tree population. An emergency appropriation was secured for the prompt removal of a backlog of infected trees, thus greatly reducing subsequent elm losses.

At the present time, Oak Park has 20,000 parkway trees on 108 miles of streets. Over 80 species are represented with approximately 300 new trees planted annually. In the future no one tree species will represent more than 15 percent of the entire tree population. This diversity will ensue that our urban forest will never again be decimated by insect or disease. *Photo courtesy of Oak Leaves*

A DAY IN OUR VILLAGE

For the past 16 years the first Sunday in June has not been just another day but A Day In Our Village, a festive celebration of people in the community with so many events scheduled in every part of the village that is impossible to attend them all.

This annual Day is the creation of Tom Steinkellner, an Oak Park resident who was disturbed by the negative coverage the village was receiving in the early 70s, as urbanologists and other "experts" confidently predicted the predominately white residents of Oak Park would flee the impending black "invasion" from Austin. The consensus was that, block-by-block, Oak Park would fall like a row of dominos.

Steinkellner decided the village needed a respite, a pleasant day when everyone would take to the streets, meet their neighbors and celebrate themselves in a day-long festival.

The village trustees agreed with Steinkellner and his supporters and gave them $1,000 in seed money. The first A Day In Our Village was a phenomenal success and in the following years the village's community relations department has taken the lead in organizing the Day.

Over the years the Day has continued to grow and provide an outdoor forum for villagers to meet their neighbors. It has also had the unexpected effect of attracting new residents to the community. Many outsiders who have come to enjoy the Day have later returned to buy homes in Oak Park.

The highlight of A Day In Our Village for kids is the opportunity to romp in front of the Euclid Avenue fire station in the foam used by firemen to extinguished chemical fires. *Photo courtesy of Oak Leaves*

A youngster with a sweet tooth eyes a gingerbread house in Mills Park during A Day In Our Village. *Photo courtesy of Oak Leaves*

Blindfolded child tries to locate the Pinata, a popular game sponsored by the Oak Park Council on International Affairs during A Day In Our Village. *Photo courtesy of Elsie Jacobsen*

Performers who staged "Raggedy Ann In Toyland" in Taylor Park during a recent A Day In Our Village have an appreciative audience. *Photo courtesy of Oak Leaves*

The 1960s were a period of great political and social upheaval throughout the entire country. In Chicago's Austin neighborhood, which borders Oak Park on the east, a wave of panic created havoc in this white middle-class community as blacks began purchasing homes in large numbers. The result was a white exodus which produced reverse segregation as block-by-block, the area changed from white to black.

Demographers and urbanologists all agreed it was inevitable that this black migration would spill across Austin Boulevard into Oak Park and property values there, too, would collapse. Those who made such predictions greatly underestimated the citizens of Oak Park, however, with their fierce community pride and "take charge" attitude when it comes to directing their own destiny.

At a time when the minority population in Oak Park was less than two percent, elected officials and citizens chose to constructively meet the challenge of integration head on. The consensus was that if change was coming, they would manage that change and not have it manage them. The full force of village government and citizen involvement would be used to change the segregated racial patterns that had devasted Austin and created a community that was truly racially diverse. The passage of Oak Park's 1968 open housing ordinance was the opening salvo in the village's fight against segregated housing. Twenty years later the village continues as a model to other communities because of progressive ordinances and programs that addressed both the economic and social concerns of integration. Whites account for 80 percent of Oak Park's current population, blacks comprise 16 percent and other minorities 4 percent. And, rather than clustering in one section of the village, Oak Park's minority population is dispersed throughout the community, confounding the doomsters who had so confidently predicted the demise of Oak Park.

To discourage block-busting, Oak Park's open housing ordinance included a ban on residential "For Sale" and "Sold" signs and also adopted an apartment licensing amendment requiring annual inspections and reports on racial counts in apartments.

To enforce this ordinance the trustees created a Community Relations Department, a watchdog agency which monitored the block-by-block racial make-up of the community, nipped racial tensions in the bud and investigated complaints that the fair housing ordinance was being violated.

In 1972 trustees unanimously passed an ordinance that prohibited the practice of "red lining" in the village. (Red lining, a type of lending discrimination by banks and savings and loans, is the practice of marking off areas in which only FHA, rather than conventional mortage loans are made — and then only to blacks. Whites attempting to break this pattern of resegregation would be unable to obtain any type of mortgage.) Oak Park's anti-red lining ordinance makes it illegal for banks and savings and loans to refuse to make loans because of the race or nationality of the person attempting to obtain a loan.

To bolster white confidence during the seventies the police force was expanded by one-third, with most of the new officers assigned to the area near Austin Boulevard, and the new $4.5 million Village Hall was built on Madison Street at Lombard in an area preceived to be "threatened."

Another positive step taken by village officials was passage of a cohesive plan for Oak Park's economic development. This 20-year Comprehensive Plan adopted in 1972 focused attention on economic development as well as integration.

A key element in the village's plan of "managed integration" was to insure the flow of funds for mortgages and rehabilitation of Oak Park's aging housing stock. Oak Park lending institutions made available to both homeowners and landlords a variety of low interest loans for upgrading this vulnerable housing and prov-

Jim and Marie Hegwood are just one of many Oak Park couples who have opened their home ot minority children for long term foster care. This 1986 family portrait includes, left to right, (seated on floor) Hoang Vuong, Hung Vuong; (on couch) Dong Nguyen, Kevin Hegwood, Jim Hegwood, Valerie Artos, Marie Hegwood and Donna Hegwood.

ing that these buildings could be recycled and made profitable.

In addition, building inspections of single-family homes and apartments was stepped up. In 1973 an ordinance requiring a "Certificate of Housing Code Compliance" was passed by the village board. This certificate is required before owners of a four-unit or larger building can sell it.

On April 9, 1973, village trustees unanimously adopted a policy statement entitled "Maintaining Diversity in Oak Park" that expressed the village's thinking and set its goals for integration.

The short but eloquent resolution says in part: "The people of Oak Park have chosen this community, not so much as a place to live, but as a way of life. A key ingredient in the quality of this life is the diversity of these same people a broad representation of various occupations, professions, ages and income levels; a stimulating mixture of racial, religious and ethnic groups. Such diversity is Oak Park's strength.

Oak Park has committed itself to equality not because it is legal but because it is right; not because equality is ethical, but because it is desirable for us and our children."

In 1976 Oak Park's efforts to promote racial diversity were nationally recognized when the community was named an All-American City by the National Municipal League. The village was nominated by the Oak Park-River Forest chapter of the League of Women Voters and selected from a field of 500 entrants who met the NML guidelines "as places where citizen energies abound."

Also in 1976, village trustees offered worried homeowners a unique guarantee called Equity Assurance which was the village's pledge to protect their home investment. Under this plan the government promises to reimburse homeowners if their homes lose value as a result of integration. All the homeowner has to do to quality is to pay the cost of an appraisal.

If the home subsequently sells for less than its appraised value and the homeowner demonstrates that racial change was the cause, the village will repay up to 80 percent of the loss. Equity Assurance was first offered to homeowners 12 years ago. Homes in Oak Park now range from $80,000 to $500,000 and no one has yet tried to claim a dime.

A network of controls and incentives helps disperse both black and white residents throughout the village. One of the most effective tools for this dispersal is the Oak Park Housing Center, a private referral service created in 1972 with two goals: assuring that blacks aren't concentrated in one part of the village and maintaining white demand for housing in integrated areas. The Housing Center works closely with the village's Community Relations Department. Both attempt to sell newcomers on the community as a whole and each makes sure that their clients understand they are free by law to buy anywhere they choose. However, if a black family wants to buy in a neighborhood where blacks already comprise 25 percent, they are asked to consider another area. At the same time, white newcomers are encouraged to do the same on a reverse basis.

In 1984 the village board passed a diversity assurance ordinance in a move to guarantee equality and diversity in multi-unit buildings. This plan gives subsidies and grants for rehabilitation and remodeling to building owners who agree to allow the Oak Park Housing Center to be the rental agent for their building and find suitable tenants that will assure the building is racially diverse. This innovative plan, like so many others passed by previous village boards during this crucial era, was the first of its kind in the country.

Fenwick, Trinity and Oak Park High School students learning to "pull together" at an annual leadership conference held for students of all three schools. *Photo courtesy of Victor Guarino*

Anton Hilton and David Richards, 6th grade students at Longfellow School, enjoy smooth sledding at Ridgeland Common. *Photo courtesy of* Wednesday Journal

James and Mary Lo and their son Charles enjoy a dinner of Chinese cuisine in their Oak Park home. *Photo courtesy of* Wednesday Journal

Andy Palomo and Shannon Hamilton display the model of the Hancock Building they made together at Hawthorne Junior High School.

Recess at Irving School in Oak Park. *Photo courtesy of Oak Leave*

The Jung family in the prayer room of their Oak Park home. *Photo courtesy of Oak Leaves*

Prospective renters and homeowners are counseled by staffers of the Oak Park Housing Center, a private referral service created in 1972 to assure that black and other minorities locate throughout the village. *Photo courtesy Oak Park Housing Center*

John Seaton, Director of the Oak Park Conservatory, 617 Garfield, shows volunteer Dan Alexander how to remove a cactus cutting for the annual fall cutting exchange. The Conservatory was completed in 1929 and is the third largest municipal conservatory in the Chicago area. The 8,000 square foot structure is divided into three permanent show houses, two growing houses and a potting area. A 35-seat classroom, the Earth Shelter, was added in 1972.

The high level of activity experienced by the Conservatory today is in direct contrast to 1970 when budgets could not keep up with accelerating costs and its demolition seemed inevitable. The building fell into disrepair but before the wrecker's ball could be called in, a group of citizens led by community activist Elsie Jacobsen mounted an emergency campaign and, in a legendary effort, led a successful drive to save this unique resource.

Today, under the direction of the Park District, the Conservatory is a flourishing asset. More than 11,000 visitors participate in its programs each year. *Photo courtesy of Wednesday Journal*

Volunteers Bonnie Craig and Lorraine Norman set up flowers for the Spring Things, the annual spring flower show sponsored by Friends of the Oak Park Conservatory. The scope of activities offered by the Conservatory would not be possible without volunteers such as these women. They produce an astounding 14,000 bedding plants for village parks each year, 3,000 cuttings for school children to take home and 10,000 plants for seasonal exhibits.

The Conservatory is a priceless community asset for villagers of all ages. Every school child has an opportunity to tour the conservatory, plant seeds and grow plants. It is also an important information center for adult gardeners offering lectures, workshops, gardening symposiums and a weekly plant clinic. *Photo courtesy of Wednesday Journal*

Hephzibah Children's Association, a private not-for-profit agency at 946 North Blvd. which has been caring for children since 1897. It was founded by Mary Wessels as a residential program for homeless children. She chose her mother's name, Hephzibah, which has a Biblical meaning of "comforting mother," for the name of the home. Today the agency is funded by the Community Chest, Economy Shop, Infant Welfare Society, grants and gifts.

A child care worker gives a youngster a boost on a gym bar in Hephzibah's After School program. In 1974, responding to the needs of single parents and families in which both parents work, Hephzibah changed its program from residential to day care for children in kindergarten through 5th grade. Today the agency works closely with social agencies, District 97 and the Park District to meet the needs of children who require after school care and full time care during the summer.

Hephzibah also provides short-term foster care to children whose families are in crisis, and in 1986 opened a 24-hour live-in program for local children who cannot live at home and whose emotional needs exceed the services of foster homes. These children live at Hephzibah for 90 days while social workers attempt to reunite the family.

Youngsters cleaning their "cooking" utensils at the Oak Park-River Forest Day Nursery. In recent years quality day care has become a top priority for many working parents. The Day Nursery, like all other for-profit and nonprofit day care facilities in the village, is licensed by the State of Illinois and meets the requirements set by the Oak Park Board of Health.

The Oak Park-River Forest Day Nursery has been providing day care since 1912 when members of the 19th Century Women's Club established a day nursery as a memorial to Elizabeth Charlton, a long time member. In 1926 the present building at 1139 W.

Randolph was completed. The Day Nursery is funded by the Community Chest, Title XX funds, parents' fees, the Infant Welfare Society and the Economy Shop.

The Day Nursery presently serves 71 preschoolers with a waiting list of 200 and is planning to open an infant/toddler program. The facility has a new motor area, participates in the Foster Grandparent Program and affiliates with local colleges and universities in student teaching and internships. *All photos courtesy of Oak Leaves*

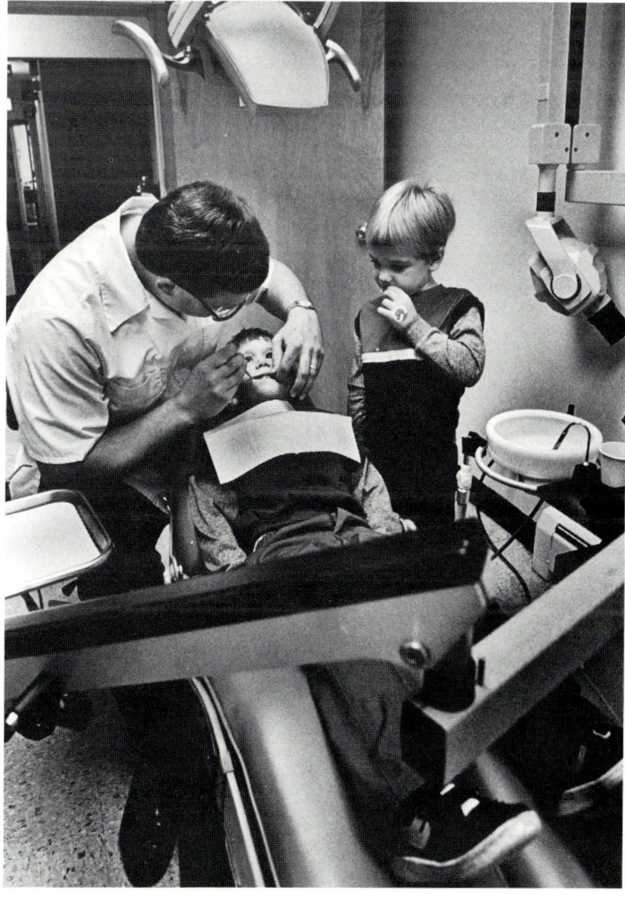

Scott Macoun, 5, looks on apprehensively as Dr. Jeff Blankshain checks his older brother Mark for cavities at the Dental Clinic, 14 West Lake Street, which is sponsored by the Oak Park River Forest Infant Welfare Society. Both the dental clinic and well child clinic provide care for infants and children whose parents are unable to budget for private care.

Infant Welfare circles have been helping village children since 1919. The Society, which helps fund almost a dozen child-related community organizations, is supported solely by the fund-raising efforts of its members and receives no local, state or federal funding.

The Infant Welfare Society annually spotlights a local home which is decorated by members of th American Society of Interior Designers and opened for tours as a showcase house every October. Proceeds from these tours fund Infant Welfare programs.

BLOCK PARTIES

For almost 20 years block parties have been an integral part of the social life in Oak Park during the summer months. Villagers know that dining al fresco with neighbors and organizing parades and games fosters neighborhood camaraderie.

Block parties were first held in the village in the early seventies as one of several activities sponsored by the Hundreds Clubs, which were outgrowths of the Area Volunteers organized under the Village Beautification Commission. But, unlike this informal group of volunteers, the Block Club system was more structured and identified with village government.

The purpose of these neighborhood Block Clubs was to bring neighbors together on projects to beautify and upgrade their neighborhoods, to provide a format for citizens to participate in decision making, and to help verity or dispel rumors.

Over the years Block Clubs have had a hand in alley art fair and alley beautification programs, in coordinating block meetings with officials in neighborhoods seethng with rumor or worry, and in get-acquainted programs for new residents.

Today the Block Club system is activated only as needed in a particular situation but the custom of holding one or more block parties a season has become a mainstay in every section of the village.

Adults enjoy catching up on the news with their neighbors in this party in the 200 block of S. Humphrey, but for kids the fun is the unrestricted use of streets that have been closed to traffic. *Photo courtesy of Wednesday Journal*

The "Spirit of '76" is alive and well in this 4th of July block party parade. *Photo courtesy of Oak Leaves*

Kids in the 1000 block of S. Wennonah entertain their families and neighbors with a skit during a block party. *Photo courtesy of Wednesday Journal*

Neighbors in the 900 block of N. Taylor congratulate mailman Bill Igeo on his retirement and present him with a farewell gift. *Photo courtesy of Wednesday Journal*

Portrait of the residents of the 1150 block of Clarence. *Photo courtesy of Wednesday Journal*

Beth Robinson, chairperson of the 1987 Book Fair sponsored by the Friends of the Oak Park Public Library, examines books donated to this annual event held every August in the south cafeteria of Oak Park High School. The Book Fair is eagerly awaited by book lovers anxious to recycle their old books and purchase new ones at bargain prices.

The 1987 Book Fair raised approximately $20,000. Proceeds from all Book Fairs are used by the Friends to supplement programs and material not covered in the library's regular budget. Both the video cassette and compact disc collections have been started with funds donated by the Friends.

In addition, Friends regularly support summer reading activities for children, film festivals, reference materials, staff continuing education and local indexing projects. *Photo courtesy of Oak Leaves*

FARMER'S MARKET

Shopping at the Oak Park Farmer's Market has become a Saturday tradition for thousands of villagers from the first weekend of June to the last weekend in October. This phenomenally successful open air market, which is held every Saturday from 8 a.m. to 2 p.m. in the Pilgrim Congregational Church parking lot at Lake and Elmwood, is an example of the cooperation between government officials and involved citizens.

In 1976 two women, Carla Lind and Marge Gockel, approached village officials with an idea for a farmer's market modeled on successful markets in Ann Arbor, Michigan and Evanston. The village agreed to provide "seed money" and space on North Boulevard between East Avenue and Euclid.

The first year the market opened with just one farmer, two greenhouses and a handful of curious shoppers. Today, between 35 and 40 farmers from a four-state area compete for space in this market which attracts 5,000 shoppers each week during the peak growing season, and showcases the freshest fruits, vegetables, flowers, plants and organically grown products.

The market is as much a social event as a shopping opportunity. Villagers flock to the farmer's market not only for fresh produce but to meet their neighbors and enjoy cooking demonstrations, bluegrass music and the thousands of hot donuts made fresh each Saturday by members of Pilgrim Church. The church, which is adjacent to the parking lot, uses the proceeds of their donut sales to help support several local charities.

Today the Farmer's Market is administered by the Oak Park Farmer's Market Commission, a volunteer group who work closely with local officials year round to provide a service which enhances the quality of life for all village residents.

Oak Park Brownie Troop 336 from Ascension School display their badges. Today one in every four girls in Oak Park between the ages of 5 and 17 are involved in Girl Scouts at five different levels. Each age level has a separate handbook that includes activities geared to that age level. *All photos courtesy of Wednesday Journal*

Hatch School Girl Scouts celebrate the 75th anniversary of scouting with songs, cake and games. Girl Scouting in Oak Park began in 1920. In 1927 the Oak Park Area Girl Scout Council was incorporated and today this Council has expanded to include 18 near-west suburbs and is called the Lone Tree Area Girls Scout Council.

Girl Scout Troop 24, Mann School, paint a mural on the underpass at Kenilworth and South Boulevard. This community service project is just one of many activities in which the girls earn badges for work completed. Other popular activities include child care, ecology, creative writing and space exploration. And, of course, all the girls still sell the ever popular Girl Scout cookies.

Jim Mullen, Carol Mullen and Leo Harmon rehearse a recent Village Players production of "Stage Struck." Village Players is Oak Park's largest and longest operating community theatre. Established in 1961 as an all-volunteer, not-for-profit corporation, the theatre's aim has been to develop creative and technical theatre skills and to provide quality live theatre to the community at modest prices. Over the years Village Players has staged over 200 dramas, mysteries, musicals, comedies and children's plays. *Photo courtesy of Wednesday Journal*

Bernie Wasmer, Rusty Padgett and Tom Higgins put the finishing touches on the "Little Foxes." Village Players owns its own fully equipped, 220-seat theatre at 1014 Madison Street, Oak Park. In 1988 over 2,000 persons have subscribed to the theatre's full standard season. Demand is also high for single-play tickets. *Photo courtesy of Wednesday Journal*

The Oak Park-River Forest Symphony Orchestra rehearsing under the baton of conductor Perry Crafton, a member of the first violin section of the Chicago Symphony Orchestra.

Crafton succeeded Milton Preves, longtime violist with the Chicago Symphony, who led the orchestra from 1953 to 1963. *Photos courtesy of Oak Park-River Symphony Orchestra*

The Oak Park-River Forest Symphony Orchestra, one of the oldest and most highly regarded community orchestras in the United States, was formed in 1931 under the leadership of Gladys M. Welge, a prominent violinist, teacher, and later conductor of the Chicago Women's Symphony.

Because of its reputation for excellence, the orchestra attracts players from a wide area. All members of the orchestra are professionally trained and have passed a rigorous audition.

A scene from a recent Oak Park Festival Theatre production of "A Midsummer Nights Dream." Oak Park Festival Theatre is the only professional company dedicated to performing the plays of William Shakespeare in the Chicago area. Its first performance site was the Westgate cul-de-sac; storage was a rented truck and a doctor's office was the first dressing room. For the past twelve summers the professional company has performed the Bard's comedies and tragedies outdoors for five or six weeks in Austin Gardens. *Photo courtesy of Oak Leaves*

Dawn Atwater and Scott Stewart preparing scenery from the Festival Theatre's production of "Julius Caesar." Festival Theatre is a nonprofit corporation formed in 1975 by Marion Karczmar to bring "Shakespeare in the Park" free of charge to the village. Early performances were subsidized by local government and federal CETA funds. The company was later forced to charge admission and become an Equity company, paying actors salaries as established through negotiations between the theatre and Actors Equity. *Photo courtesy of Oak Leaves*

OAK PARK TOWNSHIP

The newly remodeled office of the Oak Park Township, 105 S. Oak Park Avenue. Today the township, with an annual budget of almost $2,000,000, is an integral part of the community serving the needs of the elderly, children, adolescents, the retarded and substance abusers.

But this was not always the case. Following the separation of Oak Park from Cicero Township in 1901 the community was made a civil township by the Cook County Board in 1902. Since duly elected Oak Park officials were already administering the village, the township board had few duties and no taxing authority.

It was not until the Depression began taking its grim toll on villagers that the purpose and function of the Oak Park Township was clearly defined. At a time when many people found them- selves unemployed and unable to provide for their families they turned to the township for assistance.

In 1936 the electorate officially put the township in charge of the village's Poor Relief (now called General Assistance) and the township supervisor was authorized by state law to levy an annual township tax of thirty cents on each dollar of assessed valuation.

Today Oak Park Township provides General Assistance to eligible persons in accordance with state guidelines. In addition, they administer a variety of social programs including Meals-at-Home, youth drop-in centers, child care programs, mental health services and programs for seniors, which include a nutrition center and transportation. *Township photos courtesy of Oak Leaves*

A volunteer arriving on schedule with a case containing a hot meal to be eaten at midday and a lighter evening meal is a welcome sight to the homebound elderly and disabled. The food is prepared in the kitchens of The Althenheim Nursing Home in Forest Park and is delivered by volunteers five days a week.

John Insillo and Aaron Odell enjoy a game of pool at the township drop-in center for junior high students at Dole Library. Another center for teens is located at 650 W. Lake Street, just a block from Oak Park and River Forest High School.

Phyllis Erickson and Ellen Beck enjoying lunch at the Oak Park Township Nutrition Center. This federally suported center is located in Trinity Lutheran Church, 300 N. Ridgeland. Social activities at the center are supplied by Parks and Recreation Department of Oak Park

1988 view of Oak Park Avenue looking north from the North Western tracks. In the late seventies and early eighties business is this once thriving shopping district declined dramatically following the closing of two anchor stores, Wm. Y. Gilmore & Sons and The Walker Company.

Today, however, this strip shopping area is propsering under the direction of the Avenue-Lake Plaza Association (ALP), a group of area merchants. Boundaries of the ALP Association are Ontario and Pleasant Streets on the north and south, and Kenilworth and Euclid Avenue on the west and east, respectively.

An important factor in the revitalization of this area was the

1973 passage of an ordinance permitting the sale of liquor in restaurants. This ordinance ended a 100 year dry spell imposed on the village in 1873 by Henry Austin, who closed the last three saloons in Oak Park and persuaded the Cicero Town Board not to grant any more liquor licenses in the community.

Prior to this ordinance Oak Parkers were forced to go outside the community to dine and drink, but after passage of this law, an interesting potpourri of ethnic and American restaurants opened in the ALP district giving the area a new vitality.

The Goelitz Block, built in 1888 on the northwest corner of Oak Park Avenue and North Blvd., is still standing but its front facade received a facelift in recent years. Today the corner store houses Logos Book Store.

In 1980, Avenue Bank of Oak Park (right) was extensively remodeled. The bank now offers customers the services of a personal banking center on the ground floor site once occupied by two retail stores. An overhanging clock was replaced by the free standing clock (right foreground) and the sidewalk in front of the bank was bricked to harmonize with the Greek Revival facade.
Photo courtesy of Wednesday Journal

Prairie Court brings the influence of Frank Lloyd Wright to the contemporary convenience of luxury apartments. Its clean, linear roof lines, art glass windows, oak trim, red brick exterior, landscaped courtyard and lobby fireplace all reflect the spirit of the Prairie School of Architecture. *Photo courtesy of Amli Management Company*

The park-like courtyard is fully landscaped with maples, dogwoods, magnolias, lilacs, crocuses and other flowering plants. All this beauty surrounds a large fountain with terra cotta urns, fashioned after Frank Lloyd Wright's architectural style. *Photo courtesy of Amli Management Company*

In 1975 the village's administrative offices and the police department were shifted to the southeastern section of Oak Park with the completion of the new village hall at Madison Street and Lombard Avenue.

For more than ten years the old municipal building at Lake Street and Euclid Avenue stood vacant. In 1986 this historic building designed in 1904 by E. E. Roberts was razed and Prairie Court, a 125-unit luxury rental complex of efficiency one-bedroom and two-bedroom apartments, was built on the site. The cornerstone of the old village hall has been placed in a prominent spot on the Euclid Avenue corner of the complex.

This energy efficient home at 1046 Fair Oaks was built in 1981 by architect Errol Kirsch. It is constructed of synthetic stucco over a wood frame, and the narrow, angular surfaces of the exterior belie the expansive interior space. A forced air gas furnace is used to heat this unique house which contains 5,200 square feet, but the use of solar panels lower's Kirsch's heating bill to between $175 to $200 for the entire winter. *Photo courtesy of Wednesday Journal*

Building the new Oak Park Village Hall in 1975 was a milestone in revitalizing a "threatened" area and a reaffirmation of Oak Park's future. This innovative $4.5 million civic center was designed by Harry Weese & Associates around an open courtyard. It contains 74,000 square feet of interior space on three levels. *Photo courtesy of Oak Leaves*

ACKNOWLEDGEMENTS

For many years it was my goal to write a history of Oak Park. When I was given the opportunity to do so I approached the task with a great deal of interest and enthusiasm. But, however rewarding it was to research and write this book, it would not have been possible without the help and cooperation of the Historical Society, of Oak Park and River Forest and several of its members, including Sally Nott, the Society's president and the late Warren Stevens, past president of the Society.

Particular and heartfelt thanks to Elsie Jacobsen and Carol Kelm, curator of the Historical Society, who carefully reviewed this manuscript and corrected all factual errors. Both women have an extraordinary knowledge of village history and their diligence insures that this book is as factually correct as possible.

I am especially grateful to Carol Kelm for the untold hours she has spent helping me locate appropriate photographs in the Society's archives.

I would further like to acknowledge the invaluable cooperation I received from Oak Park's two weekly newspapers. I am indebted to both Carol Goddard, editor of the Oak Leaves and Dan Haley, editor of the Wednesday Journal, for allowing me to forage through their files for contemporary pictures to illustrate this book.

I am grateful to Barbara Ballinger and the staff of the Oak Park Library for their enthusiastic support. When I had a problem or reached an impasse, someone was always there to point me in the right direction.

I am also most appreciative for all the cooperation and assistance provided by Marge Richter, Marketing Director of Suburban Trust & Savings Bank.

Special thanks are also due the staff of both the Village of Oak Park and the Park District of Oak Park; to Village Clerk Virginia Cassin who provided me with a wealth of pictures and scrapbooks; to Community Relations Director Sherelyn Reid who furnished me with a great deal of useful information and to JoAnn McVey who supplied me with boxes of fascinating pictures that trace the history of the Park District.

Grateful recognition is also made to both the staff of District 97 and District 200, the Oak Park Board of Realtors, William Cassin and Bob James for their cooperation in providing me with information and photographs.

Finally, I would like to acknowledge the encouragement and forbearance of my husband, Victor, and children. As I enthusiastically shared my new found knowledge with them in the course of researching this book they all inadvertently absorbed more facts on Oak Park history than they ever really wanted to know. In a game of Trivial Pursuit on Oak Park history they would all win hands down.

BIBLIOGRAPHY

Andreas, Alfred T., *History of Cook County, Illinois,* A. T. Andreas Publishing, Chicago, 1884.

Brooke, Lee, *Oak Park's Avenue Lake Plaza,* Library Book Club, Oak Park, Illinois, 1984.

Cook, May Estelle, *Little Old Oak Park,* 1961 (privately printed).

Co-Operator Magazine, Kansas City, Mo., January, 1947.

Financing An Empire: A History of Banking In Illinois, Vol. III, S. J. Clarke Publishing Company, Chicago, 1926.

Gale, Edwin O. Reminiscences of Oak Park, Galewood and Vicinity, 1898, (typewritten)

Guarino, Jean, Docent Manual, Farson-Mills House, May, 1987.

Guarino, Jean, "The Wright Stuff," The Midwest Motorist, January-February, 1987.

Guarino, Jean, "Early Oak Park Days Captured In Pictures By Bicycle Barclay," Illinois Magazine, November-December, 1986.

Guarino, Jean, "Ernest Hemingway: Growing Up In Oak Park," FOCUS/Midwest, Volume 11, Number 70, St. Louis, Mo., 1976.

Guarino, Jean, "The Oaks Turn Over A New Leaf," Inland Architect, June, 1981.

Halley, William, *Pictorial Oak Park,* 1898, (privately printed)

Hasbrouck, Wilbert R. and Sprague, Paule E., *A Survey of Historic Architecture of the Village of Oak Park, Illinois,* reproduced and edited by the Landmarks Commission of the Village of Oak Park, 1974.

Hoagland, Gertrude Fox, ed., Historical Survey of Oak Park, Illinois, Federal Works Progress Administration Project 9516, Oak Park Public Library, 1937.

June, Frank H., Glimpses of Oak Park, (newspaper clippings).

LeGacy, Arthur E., Improvers and Preservers: A History of Oak Park, 1833-1940, Ph.D. dissertation, University of Chicago, 1967.

Nicholas, Robert, *Life Has Been Good,* Oak Park, 1962, (privately printed).

Nichols, Hi, "Pay Dirt" in Chicago, John's Publishing Co., Chicago, 1933.

Oak Park and River Forest High School, Osla Graphics, Oak Park, 1976.

Our Village: Oak Park, Illinois, Civic Service Corporation, Chicago, Illinois, 1931.

Schleden, Ina Mae, ed. and Herzog, Marion Rawls, Ernest Hemingway: As Recalled By His High School Contemporaries, monogram published by the Historical Society of Oak Park and River Forest, 1973.

Sinko, Peggy Tuck, The Suburbanization of a Community: Oak Park, Illinois, 1868 — World War I, University of Illinois at Chicago, Graduate Seminar in American History, May, 1987.

Wolf, Frances LS, The History of a Bank from 1899 to 1986: Avenue State Bank (1899-1974), Avenue Bank & Trust Company of Oak Park (1974), 1986, unpublished.

NEWSPAPERS (various issues)

Oak Park Vindicator (1883-1885, 1890-1892, 1894-1901)

Oak Park Reporter (1887-1894, 1896-1897, 1899-1902)

Oak Park Argus (1900-1902)

Oak Park Reporter-Argus 1904-1906)

Oak Leaves (1902-present)

Oak Park-River Forest World, (Ja., 1977-June, 1978)

Wednesday Journal (1980-present)

SUBURBAN TRUST AND SAVINGS BANK

BOARD OF DIRECTORS

Richard G. Pogvara, President
and Chief Operating Officer

Back Row: (left to Right) Frank Murphy, Jerome J. Brault, Richard G. Pogvara,
President and Chief Operating Officer; David J. Shaw.
Front Row: (Left to Right) George E. Jacobsmeyer, Sheldon Lavin, Vice Chairman of
the Board; Denis J. Daly, Chairman of the Board and Chief Executive Officer; Law-
rence L. Lantero, John F. Pilgrim.
Inserts: (Left to Right) Richard J. Brennan, Russell H. Ewert, Donald C. Gancer,
Robert L. Nolan

OFFICERS

Front Row: (left to Right) Lenora Bowen, Assistant Cashier; Genvieve Cortiletti, As-
sistant Vice President; Dolores Shea, Loan Officer; Michaeline Manos, Vice President;
Earl Bailey, Vice President; John Wentling, Assistant Vice President.
Back Row: (left to Right) Marguerite Richter, Marketing Officer; Christopher Joyce,
Senior Vice President and Trust Officer; Ramona Zavattaro, Assistant Vice President;
Barry Haskins, Assistant Vice President; Maria Madera, Personnel Officer; Joseph
Mack, Auditor; George Anderson, Vice President; Lorraine Smith, Assistant Cashier;
Charles Hoffman, Executive Vice President; James Teel, Senior Vice President and
Cashier.
Not Pictured: Denis Daly Jr., Loan Officer; Rae Mathieu, Trust Officer.

MADISON
ELGIN ST.
ELMGROVE ST.
WISCONSIN AVE.
MAPLE ST.
HARLEM
DIVISION ST.
FRANKLIN ST.
GROVE ST.
CLINTON AVE.
NORTH
PLEASANT
PRAIRIE ST.
EVANGELINE
R.R. AVE.
MAPLE ST.
LAKE ST.
POPLAR ST.
EAST AVE.
1 UNITY CHURCH
2 METHODIST EPISCOPAL CHURCH
3 CONGREGATIONAL
4 EPISCOPAL
5 GERMAN LUTHERAN
6 GERMAN METHODIST
BIRDS
OAK